What they're saying about this series and the authors...

"The West Orange Chamber of Commerce is proud to be connected with Mike O'Keefe, Scott Girard and Marc Price of **Expert Business Advice**. Their dynamic presentations, intellectual wealth, and unique insight into small business have helped numerous Chamber members take their businesses to the next level."

> Krista Compton Carter, IOM
>
> West Orange Chamber of Commerce Vice President
>
> Winter Garden, FL USA

"I've had the pleasure of working with Michael O'Keefe on many projects over the years. His ability to evaluate situations, identify competitive advantage opportunities and implement well thought-out strategic plans is second to none."

> Jim Costello
>
> Director of Project Management
>
> Marriott International Design & Construction Management

"Marc Price is a business builder! I have seen him start with a blank piece of paper and create a million dollar business for a financial education online application and service. He is a natural network builder and relationship marketer who works hard, is very creative, and who usually surpasses all objectives for sales, service, and market share growth. You want Marc on your team if your goal is to grow your brand and increase top and bottom lines."

> Mike Schiano, MA, CRHC, CPFC
>
> Information and Technology Services

D0910846

SALES AND MARKETING

CRASH COURSE for ENTREPRENEURS

SALES AND MARKETING

Learn What You Need in Two Hours

Scott L. Girard, Jr., Michael F. O'Keefe
and Marc A. Price

Series Editor: Scott L. Girard, Jr.

A Crash Course for Entrepreneurs—From Expert Business Advice

Starting a Business

Sales and Marketing

Managing Your Business

Business Finance Basics

Business Law Basics

Franchising

Business Plans

Time and Efficiency

International Business

Supplemental Income

Social Media

Web-Based Business

Copyright © 2012, Scott L. Girard, Jr., Michael F. O'Keefe, and Marc A. Price

www.expertbusinessadvice.com

ISBN: 978-90-77256-37-4

The Expert Business Advice trademark is owned by Expert Business Advice LLC and is used under license.

Distributed by Career Press, Inc., 220 West Parkway, Unit 12, Pompton Plains, NJ 07444, U.S.A., www.careerpress.com

D/2012/9797/2

Printed in the United States of America

20 19 18 17 16 15 14 13 12 11 10 9 8 7 6 5 4 3

Cover design: Wouter Geukens, Boris Bakker

To Bill, Ken, Tim and Scott, Sr.

Contents

Foreword

ENTREPRENEURS USUALLY ARE GIFTED in the essentials of the businesses they start. But their success can't rest on that alone. They usually become jacks of all trades, gradually acquiring a working knowledge of all the facets of their businesses.

So if you are thinking of starting a business, or have one running already, you'll understand why this book exists. If your personal strengths are in the area of sales and marketing, you'll find it a quick refresher that will help you rethink some things and learn others. If sales and marketing are new challenges for you, you'll be glad you invested the two hours or so that it will take you to read it, and you'll no doubt come back for re-reads many times in the future.

You may be doing the sales and marketing yourself, or if you have a larger company, you may manage salespeople or a sales manager—and the same for marketing. Whatever your scale of business, having a strong grounding in the thinking and practices of sales and marketing people will make you a more effective leader and do-er.

When I met Scott, Mike and Marc, I knew before they told me about the 17 businesses they've collectively started that these were talented, insightful, seasoned entrepreneurs. We quickly agreed to develop the Crash Course for Entrepreneurs together.

The aim of this series is to give you high-level overviews of the critical things you need to know and do if you want sell and market your offering in this super-competitive world. Of course, there's much more to know about every topic we visit here, but we believe that what you'll read here will give you the framework for learning the rest. A Resources section and a Glossary will ensure you can ground yourself in the essentials. And the co-authors' website, www.expertbusinessadvice.com, offers expanded support for entrepreneurs that is updated daily.

Entrepreneurs vary widely in what they want to do. Your dream may be to start a very small, one-person service, perhaps doing home maintenance or day care or accounting from your home. You may have developed or discovered a high-tech breakthrough that will need years of testing and dozens or hundreds of people to bring to market. This book sees the intrinsic value and challenges of both styles of business. It will definitely help you sell and market well, so you can make the most of your opportunity, whatever its scale.

Most of the chapters in this book represent the authors' collective experience and point of view, but a few are personal pieces. You'll find the initials of each author at the end of those. Here's a brief word from each of them.

I remember when I fully understood what our series of books should accomplish. Mike, Marc and I had only decided that we wanted to write a series of books for people only moderately familiar with entrepreneurship and business. Multitudes of books already exist on basic levels of business practices and procedures. We knew that writing another one of those books wouldn't really serve anyone or change anything, no matter how well written it was.

On the morning that I "got it," I was drinking coffee and reading the news; the television was on in the background. I glanced up and saw a commercial for a foreign language software program in which, instead of learning by simply repeating vocabulary, the student is culturally immersed in the language, holistically surrounded with concepts of all manner of things applicable to the subject. In short, they don't list facts and terms and call it teaching—they show the student a vast array of information, on a multitude of levels, allowing her to bathe in knowledge.

I knew then that instead of presenting a bunch of facts that we think you should know about sales and marketing, we should take a more holistic approach and help you immerse yourself in these critical aspects of business. Our method is most effective if you read this book cover to cover, skipping nothing. If you reach a chapter and either think it doesn't address your needs, or you think you know everything there is to know about the subject, read it anyway. It'll only take a minute—that's why the chapters are not lengthy. It will enlighten and organize your thinking, either way. You'll see important concepts woven through various discussions, as they holistically fit in.

If you're hoping to read a book and immediately become the world's greatest salesperson or marketing guru, this book isn't for you. If your goal, however, is to quickly understand and feel familiar with the basics, as your first stepping-stone to greatness, we believe that our book has no rival.

I sincerely hope that this book will not only help you to successfully sell what your company offers, but that it also gives you pleasure and satisfaction as you learn how to do it better than you ever thought you could.

Scott L. Girard, Jr.

When we sat down and decided to take on the daunting task of writing a series of books for entrepreneurs and small business owners, I cringed. I thought, "How can we ever reduce our advice and experiences to writing? And how can we cover it all—can we fit it into a book?"

Either way, we decided to get started, so each of us began drafting chapters related to our respective specialties and work experience. Only as the initiative continued did I discover a certain passion for sharing my advice in a personal way, trying to convey how it felt to plunge into selling and marketing—to plan, execute, review, celebrate or correct, and try to do even better on the next round.

I hope that this book will capture your interest, provide valuable information, and share practical, effective techniques for selling and marketing what you produce and deliver.

Mike F. O'Keefe

Everyone has heard the phrase "Knowledge is Power." *I would have it read* "Information is Power," *for a couple of reasons.*

We live in an age of instant information about every facet of our lives. We can receive news, on-demand weather and traffic reports, sports scores, social media happenings, and stock market updates. And yet, we forget much of this information within moments of receiving it, as new reports and updates are constantly replacing the data we were just beginning to process.

Most generic information travels fast these days. On the other hand, some information is meant to stay with us for a while, if not forever. And with that in mind, Scott, Mike and I set out to write a series of books to deliver lasting, valid information for entrepreneurs and small business people.

Our passion for success in business and in life lies behind every page we write. As lifelong, serial entrepreneurs, we have always taken the approach of surrounding ourselves with information, ideas and viewpoints from countless sources to support our efforts in constructing our next project. That information, when reliable and trustworthy, can and will be used over and over for repeated success. So, in essence, information is power, when applied over time.

Our series of books represents the hard work, research and application of numerous business philosophies, ideas and viewpoints. You will find rock-solid information that can be applied now… and later. It's information that can be shared, and then referred to as a refresher down the road, if needed. Our goal was to deliver sales and marketing information and advice that is relevant, smart and timely. We hope these fresh, contemporary approaches will get you, and keep you, at the top of your game.

The way forward begins here…

Marc A. Price

We all hope this book helps you translate the fire and drive you feel as an entrepreneur into solid successes in sales and marketing, day to day. And we wish you success.

Kathe Grooms
Managing Director, Nova Vista Publishing

CHAPTER I

First Things First:
Sales and Marketing Basics

The Relationship Between Sales and Marketing

Like two peas in a pod, these two have always been together. Ever wonder why?

MOST ENTREPRENEURS HAVE a common sense idea of what sales and marketing are all about, and what makes selling different from marketing. Marketing opens the gate between customers and the products or services they want; sales ensures that the buying happens. So rather than discuss the obvious differences between sales and marketing, let's focus first on the real question: how sales and marketing are connected and how, without one, the other would probably fail.

Sales and marketing are two segments of business that work hand in hand. Marketers identify customer needs, help open ways for the company to sell something to meet those needs, and try to ensure customers come back for more. If a consumer only hears about a product or service for the first time when someone is trying to sell it, the odds of a purchase go down.

So as an entrepreneur, you most likely will be spending money on marketing before you spend on sales. This is no doubt where the saying, "You have to spend money to make money" comes from.

Organizations of all sizes have to deal with this dilemma every day, because marketing is not only about introducing the product to the consumer. It's also about the prior processes of developing a brand, conducting market research to support product development, alpha and beta testing, and holding trials. The costs for these activities are incurred by all businesses. So remember, when creating your marketing plan, to budget for all appropriate marketing expenses. Then you can think about budgeting for sales.

Sales can be handled in many ways. Some companies choose direct selling. This is when the company sells its products or services directly to customers through salespeople, electronic stores (websites), or storefronts. Other companies partner with intermediaries, both nationally and internationally, who take charge of selling on their behalf. These intermediaries are commonly called distributors, wholesalers, representatives (sales reps) or brokers. Regardless of the way a business decides to sell its product or service, the sales force counts on the marketing of that product to facilitate brand awareness, brand recognition, and trust. If the marketing is executed correctly, a much better sales conversion rate should develop.

As a result, if the sales of a product or a service go well, the business will earn more and be able to fund a larger marketing budget, refueling the next cycle of the entire process.

Some companies see sales as a late stage in the overall marketing process, and the sales team may be part of Marketing. Others see marketing as supporting sales, with the schema inverted. The truth is that both models can generate excellent business, provided the two functions coordinate well. Needless to say, in a small company, sales and marketing may be done by a single person. But it helps a lot to clearly see which function is in play at the moment, so your goals are crystal clear.

Sales and Marketing:
The Winning Team

While closely related, they are not the same.
Nevertheless, never leave home without both.

SALES AND MARKETING are close to the heart of a business. Through marketing you can get clear indicators of your target market; with these, projections and marketing leads can be established. Through sales you can translate your product or service into income. Sales needs marketing to get customers; marketing needs sales to fund its operations and help move your company to the next level. *You* need both, functioning smoothly together, to ensure growth.

Marketing activities target many people, whereas selling deals with target buyers—individuals and groups clustered around some common factors. Without effective marketing, nobody will know what you offer. Without effective selling, your business has low prospects of surviving and growing. So the two functions are complementary and have equal, important value.

Marketing means all activities that are undertaken with the aim of reaching out and convincing the prospect to buy. Sales processes often involve activities to ensure that a customer buys a product, signs a contract or an agreement, or exchanges something of value for your offering.

The marketing process can vary a lot. It mainly consists of the following:

- Spotting unmet needs, a gap in the market, a new market sector where some opportunities for new offerings may lie

- Finding out the kind of product or service that will serve the needs of your potential customers

- Developing the product or service

- Ensuring that it has the attributes which meet the need of the customer

- Determining a fair price, effective name, appealing packaging and branding, and compelling proposition for the product or the service

- Making the product known to the customer

- Communicating why the customer ought to buy it (vs. the competition, or to solve a need or problem)

- Ensuring customers remain loyal, often by asking them for new concepts or enhancements on existing products, streamlining processes (think of rental cars), or building a community of users—but also offering rewards for continued purchasing

Promotion is done through different media platforms such as radio, print media, broadcast services, mobile phones, and Internet-based platforms, and includes activities such as advertising, public relations, and brand marketing. All of these are relatively distant means of contact with prospects and customers.

Another important difference is that the development and production of marketing materials, such as attractive packaging, brochures, or information booklets, is usually done before selling starts. Of course the marketing process cycles on, even after a sale is made.

Selling, on the other hand, depends a lot on effective *interpersonal* communication between the seller and the buyer. In the selling process, the level of contact between the seller and the buyer is generally high and the distance is often short. The duty of the seller is mainly to persuade or influence the customer to buy the seller's product or service, get a contract signed, or to have the customer give the seller something of value in exchange for what is being offered.

Selling is commonly done through activities such as personal meetings, telephone conversations (including cold-calling), or using contacts within the social or corporate networks of the prospect (networking) to offer the product or service to them.

The final, and most gratifying, component of the promotion and sales process is the delivery of the product to the customer, but both sales and marketing can play critical roles in the post-sale period. Finding out how satisfied the customer is, what future needs are pending (for either new things, or more of the same thing), and launching a whole new cycle are what really leverage a company's growth and success. So if you perceive the intricate intersections between sales and marketing, you can ground your enterprise in productive synergies between the two and expand your business quickly.

Creating Marketing Collateral

Always remember that people want to buy—they just don't want to be sold.

MARKETING COLLATERAL—things like catalogs, websites, booths at conferences and exhibitions—is designed to widely distribute information about your products and services. You use these things to generate sales opportunities that will bring in revenue to sustain the future growth and profitability of your business.

When developing materials to communicate about your goods or services and the needs they serve, you need to know what influences buying decisions among your prospects. This knowledge will help you to develop communication strategies that increase sales or build brand loyalty.

What's the first impression you want to create for prospective customers? You must catch the attention of the prospective customers immediately; after all, you only have one first impression, so make the most of it. Your marketing collateral should target your prospect's problem or needs, then illustrate how your offering addresses them. Your message needs to be both factually informative and enticing. The customer should be able to "get" what it is you offer with very little work. Use language or imagery in a way that ensures the prospect is both comfortable (by using appropriate language) and well-informed.

The message within the collateral basically tells the prospect about the key benefits of your product or service. Compared with an in-person selling scenario, the message in the collateral should be concise, complete and clear, so that the customer can easily find answers to typical questions: specifications, where she can find the product, price, how to order, etc. In an in-person selling scenario, you would be answering questions raised about the offering in the course of meetings and conversations, and eventually negotiating the sale.

Your materials should persuade your customers and inform them that you have something valuable *to them*. They should motivate them to purchase your product or service. You can do this by simply putting your collaterals through the following simple six-point test:

Question 1: Are you defining the nature of your product and/or service by highlighting all of the features that would interest the prospective consumer?

Question 2: Have you positioned your product or service to clearly define why it is different from your competitor? Have you touched on the pain-points that your offering eases? Why do prospects need it?

Question 3: Does your marketing material sound like your prospect? You should know how your prospects talk and think. If you don't come from your own customer base (and even if you do), you'd be wise to do a demographic study of your potential customers, including surveying the collaterals of your competitors. Keep in mind that as a result, you may find you need a couple of different versions of collaterals. A catalog company that sells toys for special needs kids may want a teacher version and a parent version, written and perhaps illustrated in different ways, to sell the same goods.

Question 4: Is your collateral easy to understand? Does it flow smoothly and logically, without causing confusion? Does it use a friendly, neutral tone? Is it uncluttered, persuasive and involving?

Question 5: Is your marketing collateral well-designed? The layout of the collateral should not only be informative, but also attractive to the eye. A home-made look may work for some kinds of business, but for many others, the investment you make to have your collaterals professionally laid out may pay you back many times over.

Question 6: Can your sales team distribute the material and know that it will pique the interest of your customers? They may not have final say on design and content, but if they really hate your collaterals you're rolling rocks uphill.

Keep these questions in mind when you are writing newsletters, advertising copy, website marketing messages, supporting collateral, and sales letters. *Always* keep your readers in mind, and *always* remember people want to buy—they just don't want to be sold (yes, we mentioned this earlier, but it bears repeating). With these important guidelines in mind, you can create marketing collateral that will lead to increased sales and take your business to the next level.

16 Marketing Tips That Work

These low-cost, highly effective marketing tips will
help you find customers and generate sales quickly.

ENTREPRENEURS HAVE so many things on their minds that they don't always take time to prioritize and plan realistically. Here are some tips that will keep you on track when you're planning your marketing.

1.   Don't expect to play right away like the big guys: Large corporations advertise to create brand recognition and future sales because they can afford it; a small business typically can't do that. Instead, think short- or mid-term and design your advertising to produce sales now—on your budget.

2.   Make an offer: Always include an offer or discount in your advertising.

3.   Set up joint promotions: Reach out to some non-competing small businesses serving customers in your market. Offer to publicize their products or services to your customers in exchange for their publicizing yours to their customers. This can produce sales for little or no cost.

4.   Seek out endorsed relationships: An endorsed relationship is similar to a joint promotion—with one big difference. The person you do the venture with actually gives you their professional or personal endorsement.

5.   Build a well-connected network: One of the biggest myths in business is that you must have a large network if you want to succeed. The reality is that the size of your network is not what's important; it's the influence of the people within your network that counts.

6.   Offer a "No Frills" version: Some prospective customers can't, or are not willing to, pay what you're asking for your product or service; others would rather pay a low price than get the best quality. (Ever seen a

$6.99 all-you-can-eat lobster feast restaurant? Same concept.) You can avoid losing sales to many of these customers by offering a no-frills, stripped-down version of your product or service at a lower price.

7. Throw your antiquated marketing guide in the trash: If you want to avoid wasting piles of money and missing countless sales opportunities, toss your old marketing textbooks and audio books in the dumpster. (Well, skim for the key concepts first.) See what's working now, and take advantage of the fact that lots of current marketing tools are free or low-cost. You can learn to use them as well as the youngest whippersnapper you know.

8. Use *Attraction Marketing*, not *Pursuit Marketing:* The most successfully marketed businesses gain the attention and interest of potential buyers by making themselves attractive. In short—they invite customers to come to them. This is where the development of a good brand will pay dividends for you. When people find a blog, page or site attractive, they recommend and forward it to their contacts, colleagues and friends. People hate being chased or pursued. Spend a day doing cold-calling and you will learn very quickly just how much people love to buy, but *hate* to be sold.

9. Offer a "Platinum Edition": While a cheaper version (see tip 6 above) will broaden the number of customers who can afford your product, not all customers are looking for a cheap price. Many are willing to pay a higher price to get a premium product or service. You can boost your average size sale and your total revenue by offering a more comprehensive product or service, or by combining several products or services in a special rolled-up premium package, offered at a higher price. As long as the higher price renders more (or better) products at a good value, someone will always be there to buy it.

10. Research your competitors: It's impossible to effectively sell or market your services unless you have researched your competitors. You need to know what offers, guarantees, prices or terms you are selling against in order to make your offering the most attractive to prospects.

11. Try some outside-the-box, unconventional marketing methods: Look for off-beat, perhaps humorous marketing methods that your competitors have overlooked. Surprise and delight people. You may uncover some profitable ways to generate sales and trump the competition.

12. Use email and text marketing: If you're not already using it, you're behind the curve. The reality is that email marketing is extremely cost-

effective and is perhaps the single most powerful marketing tool available to small businesses, followed closely by text marketing. This is because it provides predictable results and costs little or nothing to use. Here's a fun fact: text messages have the highest open rate (the percentage of recipients who at least open the message) of any marketing platform. The reason why email marketing is considered more effective, however, is because it enables you to send more info, images, links, etc.

13. Downsize your ads: Reduce the size of your ads so you can run more for the same price. You may even be surprised to find that some of your smaller, shorter ads generate a better response than their longer versions.

14. Try Internet marketing: Most small businesses are missing out on stacks of high-quality inquiries, leads, phone calls, and orders from prospective or actual buyers. They don't know that if they had a professionally designed website, one that has been search engine optimized (SEO) by a proven SEO expert, they'd have much more business.

15. Leverage keywords: Learn to make the words that deliver information on your website work for you with keyword optimization, too. It all adds up.

16. Don't mistake movement for progress: People sometimes think that the harder they work, the more successful they will be—but then, think of a hamster on a wheel! Make a conscious effort to work smarter, not harder at your marketing, keeping your goals in mind, and you will be amazed at the results.

CHAPTER II

Creating a Game Plan

How to Write a Marketing Plan

You wouldn't go on a road trip without a map or
GPS, would you? Don't drive your business in circles
by neglecting this vital navigational tool.

OLDER BUSINESSES, as well as some small new start-ups, sometimes lack a marketing plan. If you're included in this group, it's time to get to work. You snooze, you lose.

A basic marketing plan focuses on four key topics: *product, production, placement* and *promotion*. You may find it helpful to think of writing four separate, related reports which, combined, form your plan. What you are after is clarity, precision, and direction for actions as a result of your plan.

The *Product* section describes, in detail, the products or services you offer. For each item, include a detailed description, photo (if appropriate), features, costs, prices, and anything exclusive or distinguishing about it. This section can become the basis for a catalog or website listing of your offerings, an order sheet, and other documents you'll use to run the business.

Businesses run *Production* in many different ways, depending on your offering. You may do yours in house, or you may use vendors for manufacturing or intellectual property (IP) to create or provide your base materials. Perhaps you use outsourcing, private labeling, joint ventures, or licensing to create whatever you sell. If you deal in intangibles—for example, if you are a consultant, your Production section can discuss how you prepare and deliver your service. Do you license testing materials from a lab or an IP owner and then deliver assessments based on them?

Regardless of your modes of production, clearly articulate your current methods and name your vendors. Note any future production changes you plan, with a rationale and timetable. Most businesses do not use the very best choice of production available to them, either because they don't want to pay the costs associated with a change (switching charges) or because they lack knowledge about alternatives. Writing up your Production section can be a good incentive to survey providers and see if you are making the wisest picks. With facts in hand, you can have a productive conversation with your current vendors and perhaps negotiate better pricing or terms rather than switch to others.

In the *Placement* section, the information is fairly easy to create. List the locations, media and timing you will follow to release or offer your products or services. Include the reasoning behind each of these choices. For instance, here's one item from a fresh pasta manufacturer:

Item: Ravioli

Locations: Small- to medium-sized supermarkets in our city. In these markets, we will be placed in the refrigerated cheese section, because our research shows that this placement stresses freshness, and because the cheese is a natural accompaniment. Even though our freeze-drying process means we could place our ravioli next to the dried pasta in the spaghetti section, we want the premium location with the cheese to highlight our product.

Promotional Media: Flyers in mailboxes with a discount coupon in the neighborhoods within 10 blocks of the markets, in-store cooking demonstrations with samples, website recipes, maybe a recipe contest in the second half of the year?

Timing: Launch in January to 12 markets, expand to 25 by end of March

The *Promotion* section is the most subjective part of your marketing plan, and you'll no doubt have to wrestle with what you'd like to do versus how much you can fund. Sometimes, small businesses get swept away and spend money on promotions that make them feel like big-time businesses. Evaluate your spending very objectively and place targets for responses, expected sales, etc. to keep yourself from naively dropping money on gewgaws. Make sure to include the reasoning behind each of your choices.

Many specialists can assist with building the necessary collateral material to promote your offerings. Create a detailed breakdown of the different types of promotions your organization plans to use. Make sure to include information regarding print ads in industry publications, magazines and trade journals. Also, discuss handouts, event sponsorship, charitable activities, tri-folds, commercials, etc. Not all products and services need a blitz, of course, so use common sense in your planning.

It may seem like a lot of work to create a marketing plan, and in fact it can be, but it's an essential exercise. Most of your plan's readers will be employees, sales representatives and other front-line employees, or vendors or consultants who will participate. These folks may not understand the demographic research and thinking driving your marketing decisions. Your plan will get them up to speed and on board.

Even for readers who already have an understanding of your business, your plan will clarify things and show there's a "method in your madness." A well-executed marketing plan has all the ingredients to guide your marketing team in the right direction for success.

The Law of Large Numbers

*How to load the envelope until it bursts
open with results.*

DEVELOPING SALES IN A NEW CONTEXT—whether it be in a new job, career path, or business—can be a daunting task. Yet exceptional salespeople seem to glide through this initial phase, getting results in record time. The average salesperson, however, struggles. The good news is that there's a well-used key to unlock this problem.

That key is the Law of Large Numbers, and it applies to practically every kind of business, big or small, in whatever sector, whether product- or service-based. The law says that for any sales program to succeed, you need to reach enough prospects initially to account for the rather large portion of them who will not become customers. Sorry!

Consider the logic: You need a large number of initial sales contacts in order to receive enough responses of mild interest, in order to schedule enough follow-up meetings, in order to complete enough sales, in order to achieve the results you need.

The model looks like an upside-down triangle or funnel, pointing down to final sales. You may hear it called a pipeline. Depending on the experience and skill of the salesperson or the nature of a business, the actual numbers in the sequence may vary considerably.

Some say it takes five hundred contacts to yield twenty responses that will result in two or three completed sales. The numbers naturally shift when you deal in highly specialized business offerings. If you run a daycare center, your target market is urgently driven (moms and dads who need child care, right now) and often tightly localized (near home or work). Your customers are already self-qualified and motivated, so you don't need hundreds of prospects to fill an open highchair. But if you sell high-ticket or extremely "common" things, like cars or shoe laces, just think about how much higher you need to fill your funnel.

So what to do with this law? If you are an entrepreneur blessed with selling skills and a network of contacts from previous work, you may build sales pretty quickly for your new business. If you are not, you'll have to aim for a lot more initial contacts and expect a strong fall-off of prospects as you move through the sales process. There's hope, of course: As you gain experience and develop your network and skills, your success rate should go up. As with most other endeavors, practice makes perfect.

The Law of Large Numbers isn't simply a funnel, or pipeline. Quality counts. So don't spend money on an electronic mailing list of 100,000 random people to email your catalog of garden tools or to fill that empty highchair. Half of them may not have a garden or a kid! It may pay off better to buy a list of far fewer, but more highly qualified names (or hand out a flyer to each mom and dad whose child you care for, saying you have an opening). These examples are only that—you will discover much more accurately what works in your business area if you give it some thought and perhaps test a few approaches.

Your own selling skills will also play a major role in how the Law of Large Numbers works for you. If you feel shaky about your selling skills, some reading or training can help you improve your hit rate on the prospects you actually develop. Just keep the Law of Large Numbers in mind and do your planning and selling accordingly.

The Importance of
Business Networking

*It's not about exclusivity or allegiance—it's
about connections and lines in the water.
Use it, but don't rely solely on it.*

WHILE YOU MAY NOT LOVE attending business networking functions, for the good of your business's bottom line, meeting and mixing with people you have something in common with is a good thing. It's best to regard any contact you have with others as potential networking opportunities. The person next to you on the plane could become your next customer!

There are different reasons for business networking. Some people use it as a tool to meet other people in their specific industry—to learn from others' experience, find a mentor, look for talent you might someday hire, study the competition, or to stay up on news and developments in your industry. Others intentionally mix with groups of people who work in different types of industries. There could be a common interest, as for example in Toastmasters, where speaking skills development attracts all sorts of people. Or the group may share similar jobs, like quality control, but in diverse business sectors.

Some groups are straightforwardly networking driven. They may have more of a social club atmosphere, where the most common question is, "So, what do you do?" Business cards move fast, as attendees try to find out who's out there for whatever they, or people they know, might need.

Sometimes, networking groups have dues, similar to a club or union, because they offer marketing and training services to members. They may run an online database where member companies in a certain sector can buy space to advertise their offerings. Others may offer multifaceted business news, information and tools for a special interest group, like our website for entrepreneurs, www.expertbusinessadvice.com. We can automatically associate your business's search optimization popularity with ours and help you be found more easily by people who search for your industry online.

Established face-to-face networking groups have lately started to become more focused by topical interests or industry sector. When you look for one to join, choose one that will offer you the most potential for benefiting your business—which is really what it's all about. For instance, if you sell software, a networking group populated by contractors and other distributors of construction equipment is probably not the best fit for you. But you never know: They need software too.

And apart from the question of time in your day, just because you're a member of one networking group, don't feel bad about joining a few more. It's not about allegiance—it's about lines in the water. Usually people can move in and out of networking groups as it suits them. You'll be able to tell what expectations apply to the groups you are considering with a few questions.

If you don't really want to join a networking group, but want to meet more people in multiple levels of your industry, find out what conferences, conventions and trade shows are coming up. Attending as an observer first, with the possibility of exhibiting or giving a presentation in the future, is a good strategy. Or else, attend an "open" training course, one that admits participants from different companies. They can be great opportunities to make new contacts while adding to your personal toolbox.

In recent years, the evolution of technology has both enhanced and inhibited the way we approach the concept of networking. While sites like LinkedIn and others have allowed us to reach out to people in ways we never could have imagined a few years ago, they also may have diminished the status of face-to-face contact. A vital facet of networking, one that many of the world's business leaders say is the most important, is a firm handshake and a look in the eye.

We suggest using online networking sites for what they were invented for—to establish connections and to broadcast what you're about to a vast number of people. Use them as a tool for expansive research into the world of networking; just ensure that you don't rely on them as your only means of communication. While technology and the advancement of the e-universe is growing daily, interpersonal communication skills will always be vital to the success of anyone in business.

Organizing Internal Sales Training Seminars

The best way to learn is to organize and teach one yourself.

ENTREPRENEURS KNOW THAT many aspects of their businesses need to work well. Certainly, one of the aspects is your sales team. Ideally, yours is savvy about selling and ready to work tirelessly to achieve maximum profits.

If your sales team (or you, if you are it) is less than ideal, you can take some realistic steps to improve things. There is a wealth of reading materials, seminars and coaching available. But you also can organize an internal sales seminar to share and try out best practices for selling. The first step is to make such training a priority, complete with the resources needed for success: necessary materials, time allotted for preparation, training *and* follow-up, and specific, measurable goals you want to achieve by completing the process. Let's assume you have at least one person besides yourself doing sales. You can adapt the tips below for solo study if necessary.

The first step is to identify your actual needs. Why spend time now addressing closing techniques if your main problem is in getting appointments with prospects? So take time to objectively and neutrally pinpoint where soft spots or problems lie in your current sales process and the salespeople you work with, then prioritize those problems by the degree to which they inhibit sales. This will help you define objectives for your training. In doing your homework, you will find that your salespeople appreciate having a chance to speak about their desires, objectives, successes and failures. It will also create rapport and commitment to the training itself.

The next step is to plan your training. One option is to ask every participant to do a little research and come prepared to share a solution they think is worth trying, in order to address your sales problem. Or as the leader, you can do this yourself. Regardless of who does this spadework, be careful not to just scatter a bunch of conflicting approaches on the table and not have a clue about what you feel would work best. Identify the winner and work on that approach.

To start your seminar, remind participants of the problem or situation you are there to address. Invite input and discussion—this will align people on the problem-solving task. Present the solution and allow time for people to role play, write up notes to share on how they would use the new skill or approach, critique things, and generally imbed the new thinking. Work out how people will actually use this new knowledge with existing prospects and customers, and how you will measure success (SMART measures are always good: Simple, Measurable, Achievable, Realistic, Timely). Schedule next steps with responsibilities for action by name and deadline.

Successful sales training should create a positive understanding between the leader and the participants. It's good for the leader to keep an open ear to the group as they go through the training, in order to hear their views and help them understand each other. The leader should create a sharing atmosphere, yet be the chief controller of the group. This will foster equality in participation and ensure that no one intimidates other members in the group.

It's also good for the leader to be honest and open. Being open-minded is the key to unlocking the ideas of the group. Give others the chance to share their ideas or express doubts. Group members' ideas and experiences can open up discussion that will lay a good platform for learning.

Allow the group members to challenge you so that you can equally learn from them and expand your knowledge for subsequent seminars. But be prepared to put interesting but not exactly relevant ideas in a "parking lot"—a piece of flip chart paper on the wall—where a few words will help you return to that topic and do something about it later.

A big pitfall you'll want to avoid is the idea that a dose of training cures all. The secret to successful training lies in follow-ups. If you don't ensure that participants get chances (or are required to get chances!) to practice and implement what they've learned, you may as well cancel the session and prepare to live with your problem unsolved. Tell people you don't expect them to be pros at their new skill on Day 1, but you do expect them to practice till perfect—as perfect as possible.

If you do have a sales team, consider making sales training and follow-ups a once-a-month thing and have a new salesperson teach it every time. The salesperson teaching will become more familiar with the sales techniques, as he's on the spot and in the limelight, and it will also foster a team-oriented environment—one built on information-sharing and collective victory.

You can see how proper planning, execution, and follow-up are essential to accomplish your goal of organizing a successful sales seminar, just like any other task in business. Selling is hard: To compete and win sales, you need both dedication and skill. Make your sales seminar more than a one-time event. Create an experience and a process that really changes behavior and gives your salespeople the satisfaction of growth and success.

Getting Back to Sales Basics

When talking sales, everything grows from the same roots.

LATELY, I HAVE NOTICED an alarming trend in the small business arena. Many people and organizations have simply gotten away from the basics in their approach to sales and business development. They've forgotten that the *basics* are always the cornerstone to success. Let's review some of the best of them.

Establish

Potential customers are everywhere, so go get 'em! Forget all those intricate databases for the moment. Introduce yourself to people at the local coffeehouse, the gym, and at church. Hey, most of us have neighbors we've never met! Make this the time to say hello to them. Join local groups and organizations that are germane to your business. Volunteer somewhere. Lend your particular skills or expertise to someone who can benefit from it. Don't forget to reach out and get to know your current customers better, too. Get reacquainted with them and find out what's happening. Ask about changes that may have occurred since your last contact. Have their needs changed? Use some imagination, keep your costs to nearly zero…and locate some new biz in the process!

Look

Do some simple research every day. Learn about the latest market trends and read up on industry-related news. The Internet can be a vital resource for information, statistics, news on emerging products and services related to your industry, and a research device for drilling down into areas of interest. Use all of this data to formulate a plan of action for your sales and business development approaches…and gain the upper hand.

Listen

We were given two ears and only one mouth for a reason. Apply accordingly. Listen to what prospects and customers have to say, not only about your products and services, but also about the industry itself. Give them a forum to talk about what *they* see on a daily basis from *their* vantage point. They will be vital in helping you understand their needs, the current state of the industry, and even what your competition is doing. Additionally, make time to attend local seminars, conferences and industry-related events to hear what the buzz is all about in your line of work. Listen up…and you will learn a lot.

Present

Define your sales approach based on what you've seen and heard. Then, through the introductions you've made, present your products and services to not only your current customers, but to your new-found prospects as well. A strong, well-defined approach will make the presentation more direct, more effective, and better suited to the environment in which you sell. Whether it be a professional email announcing your products or services, a phone call or voice mail to introduce yourself to a prospect, or a quick pop-in to drop off a gift or noteworthy book to a customer, a confident, well-designed approach with a solid message can never go wrong.

Follow Up

So many people have difficulty with the follow-up in sales and business development. Many are too lazy or scared to do it. Others wear out their welcome by overwhelming the customer with *too much* service. The key is to look and listen to learn how and how often your customers prefer to be contacted. When you get follow-up right, you will deliver the results… and you will be on the way to serving another satisfied buyer.

Ask

This is the easiest thing to do on this list. Every customer and prospect you have knows prospects you should be contacting. Ask for a referral. Even if your buyer doesn't order this time, they may be able to point you to someone who might want to know more about your products or services. A sales lead, especially from a credible source, is money! Asking for referrals is always appropriate, if done at the appropriate time and with absolute professionalism and confidence. Social media outlets, emails, phone calls and in-person interaction can always lead to possible referrals too.

Repeat and Expand

These simple, effective approaches are entirely flexible. You can start and finish them in any time frame that suits your schedule, deadlines or industry standards. The best part is that they can be repeated and expanded upon endlessly. In fact, every sales and business development professional should have a number of these processes working at all times. There's really no excuse for not practicing these basics: They are virtually free, can be done anytime, and you can customize them for any contact or industry. So, repeat after me: Back to Basics!

M.P.

Pricing Your Products

While undershooting your target pricing would be
bad, overshooting could be worse.
Here's how to hit your target every time.

THERE ARE TWO BASIC WAYS to calculate the right price for a new product or service. The good news is that they both work. The bad news: A drastic miscalculation could level your operation. But there is other good news: It's not difficult to calculate where you need to be when pricing a new product or service.

If your business offers intellectual property or intangible services, say like leadership coaching, you still need to go through a pricing exercise. So if that's the case for you, in the following advice, simply interpret *product* as the value you deliver.

The very first thing you need to do, when calculating the price of a product, is to determine its true cost. How much will it cost you to produce it and get it to market? True cost, not to be confused with *manufacturing cost* or *landed cost*, is the most important number when pricing a product, because it's the only way to ensure that you have a "do-not-sell-below-this-amount" price. Not only must it include the cost of what it took to have the product developed and produced (more on that later), but it also must include overhead: salary or freelance fees plus any mandated taxes or benefits, freight, operations (like phone, rent, Internet), etc. All these things matter when you price something, because that's what it really costs you to run your business. In short, these costs need to be covered somehow! And then there's profit....

You can calculate your overhead cost per year by adding up all your budget lines that cover running the business day by day, and see what percentage of your total revenue it is—or is planned be, if you don't have any historical data yet. Let's say you find it's 30 percent. Then decide if you are going to load all your one-time development costs (research or design, creative work, samples, packaging, license fees or royalties, etc.) into your first year or perhaps your first production run, or if you should amortize those one-time costs over a reasonable life of your product, say three to five years. If you pick the latter approach, you'll add a third or a fifth of the development cost total to each year's product cost, divided by the units you produce during each year, to your product cost. If you're lucky, your product or service will live past your product development cost schedule, because then it will be zero for all subsequent years.

And what about profit? If you don't factor that into your true cost, you should examine your head for holes. Unless your operation really is a non-profit enterprise, you would be crazy to work so hard to break even. Naturally, you may have strategic reasons for making no or very little profit, like to capture market share initially, but just be certain you can cover that rather risky investment with future profits, perhaps from other products, to balance the picture overall.

Once you have worked out your fully loaded product cost, research the pricing of similar products on the market. Are they currently selling for less than your true cost plus profit? If they are, then that's a serious problem. You will need to find a way to produce your product for less (press or change vendors to get lower pricing, change your specifications to reduce costs, etc.) and question your overhead and product development costs. Or else, you must be able to persuade prospective buyers that what you offer is so significantly better than the competition that it merits a premium price—one which does cover all your true costs and profit.

Researching what similar products are selling for in the open market is usually fairly easy. Thanks to Internet marketing, Amazon, Overstock, and others, a product search can take less than a minute. See what others are doing, try to price your product as best you can, and see if you sell anything. The point is to do all of this rationally.

The other popular way to determine the best price for a new product is to just put the product out there and see if it sells—a more intuitive, experimental approach. If you sell a ton, raise the price. If you don't sell any, lower the price as much as you dare to. But be aware that this approach could lead to bankruptcy as easily as to a wild success.

Actually, the market will determine what your product is worth. A common misconception is that the price of a product is determined by what it *costs*. The truth is that a product is worth as much as it is *worth*. While the true cost is a good place to start the pricing process, the worth is really where the price should land. Consider that an autographed Babe Ruth baseball is technically nothing more than an old ball with some ink on it. A ball and some ink costs what, $1.50 in the US? If you had a Babe Ruth ball and tried to sell it for $1.50, you would have people lined up from here to the moon to buy it. If, however, you priced it right at $30,000 to $40,000, you would still have *someone* there to buy it, since that's what they go for these days.

While other schools of thought on pricing exist, we recommend you check out the competition, price your product close to it, and make minor adjustments up or down from there until you find the *perfect price* for your product. The nice thing about the market is that it will always tell you what it really wants.

The Magic of 99

Why a number can make or break the movement of your products.

BIG COMPANIES INVEST HUGE AMOUNTS of money in research to try to determine the right price for their new products. Psychologists have determined that the human mind is more likely to be attracted to a product priced at $0.99 rather than $1.00.

But why? It's just a penny! People walk past pennies on the sidewalk every day because they can't bother to pick them up!

The reason is because it's not the money that is enticing—it's the concept of a lower price. The concept, called *category pricing*, has shown in psychological testing that products actually sell better and faster with 99 pricing, even though it's just a penny at stake.

Subconsciously, $0.99 is better than $1.00, because although we all know it's just one cent of difference, the buyer thinks, "Okay, that product over there costs $1.00. It's not a bad price, but this other one is $0.99—I'll buy the cheaper one instead." Your eyes focus on the lack of digits before the period, so in your mind, you say that it's "less than $1.00," whereas $1.00 seems a much higher category of price. When an item is priced at $9.99, some studies say that people don't see the .99, so they unconsciously (and correctly) put it in the $9.00 price category, not the $10.00 one.

Real estate agents love to play off of the brilliance of category pricing. They'll persuade their client to list their house for $199,000 rather than $200,000. In the eyes of a potential buyer scanning the local real estate magazine, the $199,000 property will jump out on a page full of otherwise-superior $200,000 properties.

People feel good about driving all over town to use discount coupons at a half-dozen supermarkets, or go out of their way to get to the cheapest gas station.

Even though we all know that we'll probably spend that much or more in gas to do this, a lot of us still do it. Sometimes there's not a lot of logic in price-purchase thinking.

A final thought on the magic of 99: If the price of Product A is $0.99 and the price of Product B is $1.00, even if Product B has a slightly superior quality, studies have shown that more people will purchase Product A, simply because it is the cheapest option. There are actually people out there who, keeping savings at the front of their minds, would rather purchase a $0.99 product once a week, than purchase a $1.00 product once a month. The conclusion: When pricing your products in a competitive market, always remember the concept of category pricing, consider the magic of 99, and accept that buyers are funny creatures.

CHAPTER III

How to Win Customers

How to Sell Business-to-Business

*Selling your offering to another business calls
for special tactics.*

SALES EXPERTS tend to divide selling into two sorts: selling to businesses, often called B2B (as in Business-to-Business) and selling to consumers, or B2C (as in Business-to-Consumers, usually retail sales with no middleman). Of course there are more similarities than differences in these sales situations. But let's look at B2B selling, and then in the next section, at B2C selling, to see what's different but important to do in each situation.

In selling your product or service to another business, you work with a person or group who is responsible for buying for their organization. Your first challenge is to identify which companies could buy what you sell. If your business has a marketing person or group, it is likely that they have developed lists of prospects for your offerings through their marketing activities. If you don't have that resource, it is important for you do develop prospect lists yourself. The Internet, trade journals, conference or trade show attendees, and even the yellow pages (online) can point you to potential buyers.

It can be quite a creative task to profile who needs to use, and is likely buy, the product or service you offer. Try to understand the characteristics of potential customers. Remember the Law of Large Numbers (see pages 33-34) and take it into account when building your lists. But also think strategically and try to find the most highly qualified (most likely to buy) prospects you can.

Once you have a good prospect (or lead) list, complete with names, addresses and telephone numbers of the right people to talk to, you can begin contacting prospects. You may want to send some information first, then follow up, or you may want to start right away on the phone. However you do this, introduce yourself professionally and quickly explain why you are calling. Don't launch into a sales pitch now.

Instead, ask a couple quick questions about the prospect's situation and needs, as they relate to your offering. This builds rapport and demonstrates your interest in solving problems, while helping to make the prospect feel more comfortable. It also should give you valuable key words, issues, problems and the like, which will help you position your offering as a solution. Approaching a prospect this way, asking about pain points, can also give your prospect a chance to get excited about your product or service.

Another important note: be nice to gatekeepers—receptionists, assistants, or junior level employees who filter access to the person with whom you are trying to speak. They sometimes can be a source of candid information, so treat them with respect. You'll need to earn theirs if you hope to get through their gate. Be personable but professional and show you respect the gatekeeper's busy schedule.

If you must leave a voicemail message, either for a gatekeeper or your ultimate contact, make it a short (90 seconds or less), clear, concise, complete voicemail message. Stand up and smile while you do this—it really improves your delivery. Give your name and contact information clearly (even say it twice) at the end. By leaving a message, the next time you call, you can tell whoever answers that you are calling to follow up.

So far we are focusing on interpersonal skills—showing empathy, asking good questions, actively listening, developing a relationship with a gatekeeper, leaving messages. In addition, you must have good product knowledge. When describing your product, be honest; do not exaggerate or gloss over negatives. If you are frank and open, you'll increase your credibility and improve your chances of making a sale. If you sense your offering really won't suit the prospect's needs or solve her problem, don't ruin your credibility by forcing a sale.

For many salespeople, cold calls are the most difficult part of selling B2B. Like any other skill, it takes practice to be successful, so don't get discouraged if you get shot down when you're first starting out. Don't take rejections personally; your contacts don't know you. Before they learn to love your offering, you are just some person who interrupted their day. Remember that even if they decline to talk with you, you should treat them as you would want to be treated. Feel free to try new things. The worst thing they can say is *No*, right? The odds may feel against you, but with enough practice and persistence, you can find success.

Let's suppose now that your cold call worked and you get invited to present your offering in a sales presentation. This is another skill, one that needs practice and refining. If you did a good job in your initial exploration of the buyer's situation and needs, you should be able to explain how your offering will solve problems or meet needs, using the buyer's vocabulary and bringing in relevant facts you have discovered from earlier talk. With the problem defined, move on to your offering. Ensure that you focus on the positive attributes of the product first, and then continue in a descending order to other key features. Engage the buyers by giving them an opportunity to ask questions and respond to them. Don't rush. Point out and if possible, quantify the added benefits of the offering that are not factored into the cost of the product. Having done this, finish the presentation on a positive note.

A successful sales presentation thus combines interpersonal and product knowledge skills with genuine honesty. Don't be shady and or make stuff up. If you are selling a product to a distributor, chances are good that person knows more about your product and market than you do. If someone asks you a question you can't answer, just say, "I don't know, but I'll find out for you and get back to you about that soon." All of a sudden, you've shown you are honest, *and* you have given yourself an opportunity for a follow-up. Multiple meetings are good because they are added opportunities for you to get to know your customer and for them to get to know you.

By this time, you should be in a position to know whether the prospect is seriously interested in your product or not. If the interest is there, listen and note any objections the prospect may raise; respond to them frankly, and offer clarification if needed. Give your prospects confidence by addressing the misgivings or problems they have raised as objections to buying the product. This is also a good opportunity for success stories from your other customers. Sell, but don't be pushy.

If you handle that part well, the prospect may be convinced to buy. At this point, you are in a position to *close,* that is, to reach agreement on a sale. Depending on the offering you may want to reassure your prospect that what you are offering is a fair deal; explain payment options, delivery dates and details, and anything else that will follow from the agreement to buy.

After making the sale, be sure follow up with your buyer: Keep track of the delivery process, troubleshoot if necessary, and review the selling process when it's complete. By doing these things, you will get valuable feedback, which can be used for improving your marketing or offering. This feedback is also good for you as a salesperson, because it helps you evaluate your selling skills and identify areas for future improvement.

Selling B2B is very challenging, but if you apply the tips above, you will be much more likely to win the business.

How to Sell Business-to-Consumers

*Customer care can be your secret weapon in the battle
for loyal buyers.*

IF CONSUMERS ARE YOUR CUSTOMERS, then there's lots of room for creative selling open to you. A lot of it comes down to good listening and relating skills, but there's more to it than that. Let's assume you have all the basics of your business in good working order. Now we'll set the scene with a few examples:

- You run a corner bakery and coffee shop

- You offer day care for children in your home

- You sell auto parts online, only to individuals

- You have a one-person tax preparation service

- You have a fleet of taxis specialized in airport runs

If you not only provide customers the expected service or products you are in business to deliver, but also surprise them with something they value, you'll be amazed at its impact. Imagine being given a Happy Birthday cupcake on your birthday at the corner bakery. Or receiving an occasional photo on your smart phone at work that shows what your kid is doing right now at day care. Or getting an automatic 10% discount for every order of auto parts you place within a certain time period. Or receiving a funny postcard from your tax preparer to remind you to start gathering your data. Or seeing your taxi driver dashing through the rain, up to your door, with an umbrella on a rainy day. These things don't cost much to do, but help customers remember your business and talk you up with a smile.

Making it easy for customers to do business with you is also important. Your business hours, credit card and returns policies, and custom services are important influencers. In a shop filled with goods, if a clerk walks you to the thing you are looking for instead of mumbling "Aisle 4," you feel valued. If your online store is easy to navigate, the products are clearly described and presented, and the check-out process doesn't take all day, you'll get repeat business. Major companies spend huge sums to learn how to delight customers, but you can do it on the cheap too. Come up with some options you can realistically deliver, then ask a few customers what they think. There's no point in giving them extras they don't value. But if you can identify some winners, make customers happy, and enlist them as promoters, your efforts will pay off over time.

Customer service is at the core of successful selling directly to customers. Creating a friendly bridge that develops trust and shows you care about what your customer wants or needs is the foundation of this kind of business. And small actions that exceed the expectation of your customer go a long way to ensuring customer loyalty.

How to Get and Keep More Customers

Make both old and new fish want to bite with these
proven solutions.

IT COSTS TIME AND MONEY TO ACQUIRE a new customer. So a repeat customer is a big asset for your business's stability and growth. By planning your marketing properly, you can ensure that a lot of new your customers become repeat customers. It pays to think strategically about both groups.

Repeat customers

Happy customers keep coming back. The first step to increasing your repeat business is to understand what fosters it. Analyze your strengths so that you can replicate them. Repeat customers come back for a variety of reasons, including convenience, high switching costs, tradition, a feeling of loyalty, and unique personal motivations. Mostly, though, they come back to you because of something you do better than your competition, or because you do something that your competition isn't doing at all. Once you identify your strengths with repeat customers you can leverage them on new ones. Ask yourself these questions:

- Why are these customers continuing to buy from you?

- What are you doing pro-actively to keep them coming back?

- What advantages do you have over your competitors, in their minds?

- Have you consciously built rapport, loyalty or friendship with them?

- Do you have mechanisms for learning about their questions, desires and concerns?

- Are you taking their input into consideration?

There will be a lot of things to think about and do as you come up with answers. They will help shape your marketing plan for building this sector of your customer base. Here are a few practical tips:

- Start sending thank you notes or making thank you calls for your existing customers to let them know you appreciate their business.

- Launch a "valued customer survey" to get input on products, pricing, marketing.

- Plan a customer appreciation event—how about an open house at your business, an activity linked to your business, a contest?

- Reward repeat customers who tell a friend about you when that friend becomes a new customer.

- Offer loyalty program incentives: a point system that yields a discount or gift when a certain level or frequency of purchases is achieved, a members' club with special benefits, and so forth.

- Encourage word-of–mouth advertising, the best way to market your company.

You need to be very well informed about your existing customer base so you can expand it. Look at who your current customers are and rank them according to the profits you are generating from them. This will help you see what kind of prospective customers you should focus your attention on. You may have a group of very reliable customers, but you need to focus on the ones who are both loyal *and* make your profits grow significantly.

Equally important is your knowledge of your competition. Get on their mailing lists and keep yourself updated on their developments and new promotions. This way, you will never be left to wonder how you stack up against them in your marketplace. Their customers can become yours someday!

New customers

Acquiring new customers doesn't happen instantly or without a solid marketing plan. Often, in a small business, you can't launch a marketing plan for new customers and still maintain peak performance with your repeat customers. Below are some inexpensive ideas that can help to acquire new customers *and* maintain repeat customers:

- Try printing new flyer ads and expanding the territory where you distribute them.

- Have a sale or promotion on products that aren't moving.

- Create coupons to stir up new business or entice existing customers to continue shopping with you.

- Make them aware of special promotions and/or discounts that you have going on for the day, month or year.

- Maintain regular contact with your customers with email blasts of promotions and discounts.

- Use public relations to your advantage by having a television or radio station do a story on your business. Also, consider using a highly circulated newspaper or magazine to do the same; this will give immediate third-party validation and exposure to your company.

- Join one or more networking groups and make connections.

- Use social networking sites like Facebook, Twitter, LinkedIn, Google+ and MySpace to make people aware of your business.

The value of reputation, reviews and such is an important factor in acquiring customers. In a recent study,

- 72% of respondents checked out a company's reputation on chat boards before buying (e.g., Homeownersplaybook.com)

- 74% based their buying decisions, at least partially, on what they had read

- 81% thought that blogs, online rating systems, and discussion boards gave them valuable feedback

So perhaps the hidden value of repeat customers is that they are your front-line marketers. Their promotion of your company can be a key element in your business's ability to find new ones.

Five Basic Ways to Advertise Your Business

While creative business advertising is great, don't forget these proven basics for a solid marketing foundation.

BUSINESS OWNERS OFTEN BYPASS some of the most basic fundamental advertising methods when attempting to promote their business. Before the budgets and the brainstorming sessions get overrun with wild ideas and strategies, be sure you consider using one or more of the five most common, yet extremely effective, advertising methods. The nature and size of your business will help you select methods that are most likely to produce profitable results.

One of the most beneficial initiatives for a business is running regular *print advertisements* in newspapers (local and national), industry-specific magazines, or trade journals. These publications typically have large reading audiences and they tend to be read by members of a particular niche or target audience. The costs associated with running print ads can vary greatly, depending on the size of the publication, the number of readers, and the frequency of your ads. Obviously, the more a business is willing to commit, the deeper the discount off of the standard rate card.

Another worthwhile initiative is a *direct marketing initiative*. You can either conduct research and compile a marketing list yourself, or purchase one from a source. These lists typically contain pertinent business information such as the recipient or business's name, address, phone and fax numbers, and emails. This information can be used to launch a mailing that could include something as little as a postcard or as comprehensive as product or service catalogs and other related business information. Just remember, postage may seem inexpensive, but when you directly mail 10,000 businesses or consumers, your postage alone will be significant. Then, you have the costs associated with developing the marketing piece and printing. Luckily, most of this can be contracted out to one or two businesses that will acquire the list, develop the piece, organize the printing, and oversee the mailing. These types of firms will typically only need you to approve ideas; other than that, they can do most of the heavy lifting.

It's important to remember the Law of Large Numbers when you consider a direct marketing initiative. A list of 10,000 qualified names may deliver 2% responses (not orders) if it's quite successful, in some kinds of business. That comes down to 200 responses, which you then get to contact, make your pitch to, and hopefully sign up a new customer. You wouldn't want to invest the necessary time and money in this mode of promotion if you have a small frozen yogurt shop! This approach would be more useful for a frozen yogurt franchise that is seeking 50 new outlets, each paying significant money each year to your company.

On the other hand, don't underestimate the value of *business directory listings*. Business directories serve a very basic function but can be extremely effective, especially if the business directory is read by consumers of your product or by individuals and businesses who make up your target audience. Most business directory listings are inexpensive when compared to other marketing initiatives, such as print ads, direct mail, websites, radio and television, or even going to tradeshows. The average cost of a business directory listing in the US is between $100 to $1,500 dollars per year. That may seem like a lot, but if you break it down to a daily expense, it becomes reasonable—if it works. So if you can list your business on a business directory or multiple directories at reasonable rates, consider doing it. The potential targeted exposure can be huge.

Internet marketing is another option: In its most common form, you bid, offering the top price you want to pay on keywords that pop up as people search for information online, and if the searcher clicks on your ad, she is directed to your website. Pay-per-click ads allow you to pay only for the times people literally *click* a link and are directed to your website. It's easy and manageable, because you can set a maximum budget, along with daily budgets, that you agree to spend. That way you can get the most out of your campaign. Best of all, the entire campaign is customizable. As the administrator of the initiative, you can choose to show advertisements on certain keywords or phrases, and you can create, update or remove advertising messages and display texts. Most Internet marketers agree that these campaigns can be very rewarding to businesses that dedicate the time and resources to achieve the best possible outcome.

Radio and television are both valuable media outlets because they reach a large number of consumers and business personnel on a regular basis, and advertisements can be strategically placed on stations and at times (e.g., during specific programs) that draw a fairly targeted audience. The only downside is that radio and television commercials are quite a bit more expensive than other types of advertising media and they can cost a lot of time and money to put together. The complexity can really slow down the speed of a marketing campaign; therefore, it's important to create a timeline with milestones and deadlines to successfully manage the project from start to finish.

These five basic types of advertising comprise the majority of the efforts made by most medium-sized and large businesses. Some, like Internet marketing, work well for small businesses and start-ups and are not necessarily expensive. The key is to target the right potential customer base and deliver an effective selling message.

Public Relations and Publicity

A business's interaction with the public is vital, but doesn't have to be expensive.

THERE ARE NUMEROUS WAYS to help not just the general public, but also your target audience, find and learn more about your business. It's not that one is more effective than another, but certain initiatives can be more costly and time-consuming than others. When individuals think about public relations (PR) in business, they typically envision spokespersons and media campaigns building brand, product and service awareness. This is true, in part. However, there are several ways to actively build a level of brand-consciousness with your business's target audience.

Write articles or books. This helps build credibility, gets your business's name out there, and gives you a platform to air your views, product news, and so forth. If it's well written and useful content, you may even be able to get your content syndicated within your industry—typically through trade journals, magazines, and websites.

Create press releases. These are beneficial because they can be sent out directly to media outlets such as web-based press release sites and specific industry news sources. as well as the traditional press. It's wise to do this regularly, as you never know when something your business is doing will be considered newsworthy.

Website. It is absolutely essential that a business have a website to help viewers from all over the world learn about them and their products or services. Entrepreneurs realize that the number of consumers using the Internet to seek out potential product and service providers is rapidly growing every year, and their presence online puts them on equal footing with established companies. As computers become less expensive and Internet access becomes more readily available, doing research on sources of products and services is becoming the standard, for many reasons. It costs next to nothing, there is no travel, and if the business offers online shopping, customers can purchase from home or the office, never having to deal with traditional brick-and-mortar stores. Even if your business is a brick-and-mortar enterprise, you must be visible and accessible to the buyers you seek via your website.

Newsletters. Here's another no-brainer. You simply create a sign-up sheet for your physical business place and make another electronic sign-up on the business's website. Once you collect contact information from interested parties, you can update the group regularly with news, product or service updates, and upcoming events.

Non-profit support. These groups are always looking for help and money, and a business can aid a cause (and get some publicity) in many ways. You can make a financial contribution, or you can provide your products and services to the non-profit organization free of charge. Both kinds of support make your business look great, give the non-profit valuable assets, and can benefit your networking process.

Certifications, awards, ratings and honors. This is basic stuff—the more awards, ribbons, gold stars, etc. your business wins, the more qualified and credible it will seem in the eyes of your target audience.

Secrets of Sales and Marketing Strategies

*How to create, change and ensure success of your sales
and marketing plan.*

CREATING AND IMPLEMENTING a new sales and marketing strategy is often considered a tough job, say compared to the development of a prospectus for a new product. You may need a new one because of one of these scenarios:

- You need to generate higher sales

- You need to sustain current sales volumes

- You must recover from the failure of a previous plan

For any of these scenarios, it is important to ask yourself what things need to be done differently to yield the sales impact you want. It's also important to get input and feedback from the people who will execute the plan. You may need to take the lead and rule out some things, but your team's support, practical perspectives, and ultimately their engagement in carrying out the plan are critical to its success.

Working with your team, draft a list of the new things that you wish to try out in your new strategy. Attach costs and results (even if only ballpark numbers). Choose and prioritize the ones that the team feels are the most promising. It can be helpful to review what remains unchanged, to ensure the whole strategy works smoothly.

The 8 Ps can guide to through the exercise of deciding what needs to change when selling your product or service.

- **P**rice: Ensure yours is competitive with your current competitors.

- **P**roduct: Ensure that your new item actually satisfies a market's desires or need.

- **P**romotion and advertising: Focus on getting the offering well known in the marketplace.

- **P**lacement: Focus on where the offering is located and/or seen.

- **P**eople: Represent the business and deal with customers in a positive and respectful way.

- **P**hysical environment: Focus on the ambiance, mood or tone of the environment. This will help your customers feel comfortable and want to continue buying from your organization. Make it pleasant to buy.

- **P**rocess: Consider and focus on how people will obtain your offering in a stress-free, efficient flow. Make it easy to buy.

- **P**ackaging: Focus on how the product will be protected and ensure is it aesthetically pleasing and environmentally responsible. Like it or not, packaging is a very large reason why some people may choose your product over your competitors'.

Once you have established what to do differently, decide how to test the new strategy. Establish concrete indicators that will be used for monitoring and evaluating the effectiveness of the new strategy. In addition to the obvious one—sales growth—you will want to apply deadlines, milestones, revenue targets, and the like.

Because information and communication now travels in so many ways, you will probably need to make decisions regarding the types of platforms you will use to implement the new marketing strategy. Such platforms may include brand activations or integrating new forms of advertising. Don't be afraid to test new platforms that were not incorporated in the previous plans. Among the emerging platforms, for example, web-based social network marketing and mobile marketing have delivered more than traditional marketing tools, such as print media, in terms of reaching a larger number of people and a corresponding increase in the volume of sales.

There may be pricing, payment terms and delivery conditions that can enhance sales too. Studies have shown that if you can compete with your competitor and offer a price that is 20 percent lower than theirs, the customer will switch over to you. Giving a discount for early payment can be attractive (if it doesn't harm your own cash flow too much). Or delivering goods or services in "chunks," with staged payments attached, may convince customers to take on larger buying commitments. Whatever you choose to do, to achieve maximum impact, the plan must be clear, concise and simple.

To support the new strategy, people responsible for sales should make an audit of the human resource capacity of their sales team (whether internal or external). Managers should look for the qualities, skills and capabilities among their existing sales staff that will be needed to make the new strategy deliver. Some of this could be technical knowledge, particularly if you are testing new platforms. At times, it is necessary to train experienced staff members on new selling techniques. And for some initiatives, you may need to bring in an entirely new skill set. That may be done through hiring new people or outsourcing certain responsibilities.

Experience points to these three important elements in successful new sales and marketing strategies.

- The first is to allow creativity and innovation to flow freely. As previously explained, the failure of a strategy can be attributed to using only tried-and-true marketing or selling techniques, which though relatively effective, do not give the business the leverage it needs to beat the competition.

- The second is proper planning and paying due attention to the execution itself. This increases the chance that all activities will be carried out as intended. Make sure that timely feedback gets to the right people so they can monitor, correct and report results to decision makers.

- Lastly, *sustained* focus is needed to make any sales and marketing plan a success. As a leader, don't make the common mistake of announcing the new strategy and then moving on to focus entirely on the next challenge. Keep reminding everyone involved about how their actions fit with the larger plan and proactively re-direct misplaced activity.

The 80:20 Rule applies to sales and marketing plans too. Generally it's true that you need to concentrate on the top 20 percent of products or services, and the top 20 percent of customers, that will account for 80 percent of the sales volume and 80 percent of the profit.

While every business is different, in general, regardless of you offering, this model will help you. It's worth making it a high priority when you take the challenge on.

Creating Leads

In sales, the Law of Large Numbers says that the more leads you start with, the more you sell. But there's more to it than that.

VIRTUALLY EVERY business must market itself in order to survive the stiff competition in today's global marketplace. That is why you will find someone wearing a marketing hat in even very small businesses. You might even say that leads are even more important to a small business than to a larger one, but the fact is that leads matter to everybody.

The traditional way to generate leads—names of prospective customers— is to buy or develop a list of likely prospects and contact them. You'll probably want a large number of them, but the quality of the leads is ultimately more important than the number, even given the Law of Large Numbers. After all, if your list of five extremely highly qualified leads points you to three new customers who buy tons of stuff from you, you can take the day off. If a cheaper, less targeted list of 10,000 names yields the same, you may still take the day off, but you also may have wasted more resources getting them culled out.

Your business may respond well to leads generated by mass media—including newspapers, radio, text, and television, among others. You will obviously be charged to use these channels, but you certainly will touch a large number of current and prospective customers. You do not need to approach the mass media yourself, because various marketing and advertising companies can do this for you. When you define what you are after, and agree to the fees and prices involved, they will execute your leads generation campaign using appropriate forms of mass media. Most firms offer guarantees of response rates, but in general, you get what you pay for. Discount mass media campaigns will often find your ads in wastebaskets, bulk mailboxes or blocked by corporate firewalls.

Since the advent of online marketing, businesses today combine traditional lead generation strategies with Internet strategies to re-activate existing customers and identify new ones. Most big businesses develop leads using social media, radio, newspapers, and television simultaneously, so as to harvest leads from every available source.

Whether you literally do it yourself, or you have an outside firm or your in-house marketer do this work, make sure you get the best talent and track record you can afford. This is not a job for amateurs. For outside vendors, get names of their current customers and probe those customers for the results of their projects with the firm, both in terms of numbers and quality of leads. Only use experienced sales and marketing people in house for this job, and consider hiring an outside firm to consult with your marketer until he or she is performing well.

Here are some of the techniques employed by various businesses and lead generation groups, as well as a discussion of the importance of such groups in business.

Leads can be generated via the social networking sites on the Internet. Sites like Facebook, Twitter, Google+, LinkedIn, etc., give you places where you can market your business to their frequent visitors. To generate leads from these sites, your business must be an active member of the site. You must participate by publishing articles and placing ads and links to your website on these social sites in order to familiarize people with your business and offering.

Your business may sell something these visitors can buy instantly from your website, like shoes or a week at your holiday rental property. To convert such leads into sales, be sure your site is ready: Can a visitor see right away what you do? Can you securely accept online payments? Do not require people to provide unnecessary details when they visit the website and make sure ordering is easy and fast.

On the other hand, maybe you are selling power plants. A list of 20 buyers may lead to one proposal and one sale, but that's the way your type of business runs. Leads from the social media may still help you, but it's likely that you'll get floods of the wrong names. So make sure you fully understand what your own goals are and that you have expert guidance to display your company and its output in front of the *right* people.

Since many people today shop online over the Internet, ensure that your business's website is ranked on top or among the top of your category by the Search Engine Optimization (SEO) companies. This may come at a cost, but it is a sure way of generating sales leads. Research conducted on on people browsing the Internet found that most of these browsers never go beyond the first page of their search engine website (Google, Yahoo!, Bing, etc.) when making a general web search. This means that if your business's website does not appear on the first page of a search engine, you probably won't have many people visit it, and thus, not generate the leads you want.

You can also generate leads through Internet affiliate programs. This is a fee-based strategy where visitors to other (usually related) websites will be linked to your website when someone lands on those related sites. Web visitors who want more information on what they are researching are more likely to get it from the related searches rather than initiating a fresh Internet search.

Many businesses now use Facebook, which is the most frequently visited social networking site, to form a business group. In Facebook terms, a business group is simply an information page on Facebook, hosted by a given business, that provides followers with information related to the business. You will need Internet experts to create an effective business group there. Many online advertising and marketing companies have sprung up; these companies can advise on how to successfully generate online leads. But as with more traditional lead generating firms, check their credentials and references carefully.

The bottom line: You must be prepared to spend money in order to put your business ahead of competitors. Always seek fully qualified professional advice, whether you work with traditional or online methods, whenever you want to generate leads. It really is true that you get what you pay for.

Creating a Referral Network

The goal is to acquire and keep customers. Why not be creative and put your business contacts to work for you?

MOST SOLO ENTREPRENEURS feel alone and perhaps a bit overwhelmed when they try to think of ways to acquire more customers. They know it's critical for their business's survival and growth to attract and retain customers. And they expect that if they can acquire new customers fast, many of their business's other challenges (cash flow, for instance) will ease.

We know what you're thinking—easier said than done. In many start-ups, the owner is both the sales and marketing department (as if she didn't already have enough to do). That puts a lot of pressure on her. However, there are proven ways of creating a happy and willing group of people who stand ready to refer prospects to you.

A referral network is a group of people who know you and understand your business. They go about their own business, but watch for opportunities to refer prospects who could be interested in purchasing your offering to you. Usually these networks are reciprocal—you'll be expected to refer opportunities to them as well.

This approach can start a free, potentially rich flow of prospects who are already positively inclined toward you (thanks to the endorsement of your referring colleague). It makes the sales process run faster and smoother, bringing in revenue and enhancing your other sales activities.

There are a couple of types of contacts you can set up a network with. One is a business which is in the same general business sector as yours, but which operates in a different market niche. For example, if you have a lawn services company, you might approach the local greenhouses and leave a supply of business cards and brochures with them. Or if you design and sell a line of baby clothes, you might connect with other clothes designers who specialize in items for school kids.

A different approach is to think about contacts who themselves have contact with people who'd make good prospects for you. Your banker, dentist, golf club pro, or even your babysitter may hear from one of their customers that they need just the widget you make!

A third approach is a bit different. It's a kind of ad hoc partnership between you and someone whose business complements yours. Say that you teach Spanish to executives, one-on-one, during the business day. You know someone who teaches Spanish in classroom settings. By teaming up and making a pitch to a large company that needs Spanish courses for both their execs and other employees, you can create a credible proposal that makes the most of both your strengths and exactly delivers what the prospect wants.

The key to a successful complementary referral network is to focus on developing relationships with businesses you truly believe in. The primary question you should ask yourself is, "What can this partnering bring to my customers?" rather than, "What can this partnering bring to me?" This will help you to create joint offerings driven by the needs of the customers.

Some people are hesitant to ask for referrals. They see it as close to begging or cold-calling, or they fear rejection, killing the referral process before it even takes off. To manage these feelings, just think of the number of customers who have been satisfied with your offering. Of course they will be willing to recommend you to others. And ask yourself if you would mind referring business to a contact of yours. Wouldn't you do that gladly? Assuming someone will feel reluctant to help doesn't give that person a chance to decide for himself.

Approaching this strategy positively and proactively also helps a lot. Picture yourself chatting with a potential network member. Ask, "Can we set something up so that if you hear about an opportunity for me, or I hear about something for you, we recommend each other?" Or, if you think an ad hoc partnership might work, ask, "How can we partner up to get some business together, based on our complementary offerings?" Asking for referrals instead of waiting for them to spontaneously happen gets things moving faster.

Planning and even writing down what you want to say when asking for referrals helps, too. Just like in an interview, you may not be comfortable in saying something new, but by writing and memorizing it, it becomes part of your routine.

The best time to ask a *customer* for a referral is when you have received a compliment or when you've delivered your offering. A compliment is a natural cue to ask whether your satisfied customer knows somebody else who needs your product or service.

Some referrals are just informal tips. Others can get quite complex. Depending on the situation, a simple thank you, a lunch invitation, or a thoughtful gift may be all that's needed to show your appreciation. If you stand to win substantial gains, or the referral is an in-depth, complicated affair, a greater reward is in order. Some businesses create a referral program where customers end up receiving a referral discount or a gift for every customer referred to you by them. For large-scale referrals, the parties may work out a "finder's fee," where the person who referred the business might get 10 percent of the first year's profit. You probably can afford to be generous with your rewards, because you didn't invest much to get the lead and the business is "gravy" you would have otherwise missed. If significant money is involved, document exactly what the reward will be, preferably before your network goes into action. If people know what's in it for them, they'll think of you more often. The incentive pays off.

Any enterprise is capable of benefiting from a referral network. It doesn't require in-house salespeople and can cost little or nothing. If you build your own referral network, your business ultimately benefits in two major ways: You'll see an increase in leads, and when you talk to your own customers, you can mention the additional resources that your network partners offer, which may make a more complete sale package. Your customer will appreciate your thinking of his needs, and that may make future sales of your own offering easier. And finally, it's not so lonely when you have a referral network to touch base with now and then.

Asking for Referrals from Current Customers

An acceptable fringe benefit of doing a good job is having the opportunity and confidence to ask for referrals from your customers. Here are the rules.

WHEN YOUR CUSTOMERS refer you to others, it's a huge compliment and a great opportunity for you to build up your current customer portfolio. It doesn't cost you anything and leads to very easy sales, since the person who referred you is highly trusted by the prospective buyer.

Typically, friends refer to friends, and since your customers can testify to the high level of quality of your products and services, they would want to refer you to people they know and like. Most businesspeople do not spend their time asking for referrals, they just worry about where and how they will get them.

There are several ways that you can get continuous referrals without having to go asking for them. Below are a few helpful tips:

- Start by listing the people you consider valued customers and who do business with you regularly. As most people may not help you acquire more customers out of the kindness of their hearts, you must incentivize them. Talk with a few and ask what would make it worth their while to provide referrals—a small fee? a discount on their next purchase? The reward must matter to them.

- Ensure that each time you get to speak with a prospect, you let them know that referrals are a main source in growing your business. Even if they don't buy, they may suggest others who are in need of your services.

- When giving out your business cards or brochures, consider giving the customers extra in order to give to their friends or colleagues who they think may require your offering. Also, when having new cards printed, consider adding a statement like, "The highest compliment our customers can give is to recommend us. We appreciate your referrals!"

- The best time to ask for a referral from one of your current customers is immediately after completion of a task or project. If the customer is pleased, ask if he knows anyone else you can contact. Another, less up-front way, is to simply ask your customer to keep your name in mind when talking about the job or project with his colleagues.

- While asking for referrals is best done face-to-face, it's not advisable to ask for a referral when you are presenting a bill to a customer, as no matter how great your work is, most people aren't in the best of moods at that time. Conduct a follow-up call the next day to thank them and let them know you appreciate their business. From there, ask if they would be willing to provide you with names of appropriate friends or associates that you can contact, using them as a reference.

- If you succeed in winning business from someone you were referred to, contact the referring person again and let them know that you appreciate it (whether or not you have a reward program in place). Chances are, the older and new customer have been in touch about your work, so it's nice to close the loop and make this thank-you gesture.

The bottom line is that referrals are earned thanks to a proven track record of doing good business. Satisfied customers can help you create more of them, so don't ignore this valuable source of new business.

Escaping the Fear of Cold-Calling

The monster in your closet wasn't scary when you discovered he was just a pile of old clothes. Years later, the same rule still applies.

A LOT OF PEOPLE ARE AFRAID of walking up to a complete stranger and starting a conversation. Why? Because they fear rejection, embarrassment, confrontation, intimidation, etc.—or they think maybe the stranger will turn out to be just plain horrible to deal with. In theory, cold-calling has the same risks, but you can turn your fear into a skill with a few insights.

Cold-calling typically refers to the first telephone call made by a salesperson to a prospective customer. But it can also refer to visiting commercial premises or households for the first time without an appointment. It is a vital stage in the sales process for some businesses.

Some of the skills that successful cold-callers use serve them well in many other aspects of business and life. The ability to approach a stranger professionally, openly and meaningfully, with a sensible and confident proposition, is very valuable. Most great entrepreneurs and leaders possess this ability—or they wouldn't have become as successful as they are. In fact, it is the preferred approach of a lot of entrepreneurs, and the reason most entrepreneurs elect to start their own businesses. They recognize that the best opportunities are new ones, and they are so heated and passionate about their business that they don't sense the "cold." To them, cold-calling welcomes and makes the most of a blank sheet of paper. They get to put their individual stamp on things.

So for entrepreneurs, cold-calling is the key to opportunities and personal achievement. Rejections cease to be the problem. Resistance ceases to be insurmountable. Obstacles become steps toward success. They think about the contact through the eyes of the prospect, and they love being creative as they go about it. Take a lesson from this perspective, and in your cold-calling, try to be inventive—to see beyond the script, beyond, "That's the way we've always done it."

Unfortunately, there isn't a magic script, despite a wealth of books and training offering helpful outlines and methodologies. Successful cold-callers view it as a game rather than a chore or a conflict. For them, it opens business opportunities that are new—free of baggage and history, and not weighed down by any previous expectations. The possibilities are endless and unforeseeable. Somebody might respond; maybe one in twenty, maybe even one in a hundred. Then you get to see what happens when the door opens.

Even when following a script, a gifted cold-caller watches for the opportunity to improvise and try out new strategic ideas and styles. If they work, they can be extended into initiatives and campaigns for others to follow.

So get that monster out of your closet and find your own approach to make cold-calling work for you. You'll be glad you did.

Why is Cold-Calling So Difficult?

If it were easy, everyone would do it. Once you've accepted that, you can use it to your advantage.

AS WE HAVE seen, cold-calling is often considered the most challenging aspect of selling. And it is becoming increasingly so. Prospects' time is precious and they are harder to reach directly. When you do connect, they are more likely to quickly decline to hear or see you. The uphill battle is becoming steeper.

The typical salesperson feels extra pressure when cold-calling. She may project that stress when talking to her prospect, which can make the prospect feel pushed and defensive. Any hope of developing meaningful trust is lost, and recovery is essentially impossible. Still, salespeople who embrace a positive and skillful approach to cold-calling generally find it gets easier with practice and experience.

If cold-calling were easy, everyone would do it. Our advice: try some role-playing and brainstorming exercises so you'll have some effective replies when prospects give you reasons why they're not interested in talking. Successfully handling these challenges before you make contact leaves you ready to focus on the business opportunities at hand. In New Line Cinema's *Boiler Room,* one of the characters tells his unsuccessful salespeople,

> There is no such thing as a 'no sale' call. A sale is made on every call you make. You either sell the customer some stock or he sells you a reason he can't buy. Either way, it's a sale. The question is: who's going to close—you or him?

You may notice an overwhelming theme of not actually *selling* during the cold-calling process. A conversation may or may not be possible. People will hang up on you, be rude to you, and may even curse at you. Don't get discouraged, and certainly don't take it personally. After a handful of calls, you become immune to it, and you'll be able to move on to the next call like nothing ever happened. Just keep in mind that, generally, the purpose of cold-calling is simply to open dialogue, make a connection with that prospect, and to get permission to send materials or make an appointment. If you don't make an appointment, but you were memorable and you delivered your message accurately, at least you made your prospect aware of your company, and that's still a huge step in the right direction. You never know, in the near future, they might need your offering and call you back.

Here are a few more tips:

- If possible, do your cold-calling for a fixed period of time each day, rather than doing whole days of it. You'll be fresher, more positive, and it won't seem so daunting.

- Get permission to send something about your offering. If things are going well in that first call, you can call again to confirm the materials were received and ask for a response, hopefully a step further down the sales path.

- If you get a rejection, and the tone is okay, ask if your prospect can point you to a colleague (inside or outside her organization) who might be more appropriate for you to talk to.

- As we've said before, stand up and smile when you call. It warms up your voice and reduces your tension.

- When possible, simply avoid totally cold cold-calling. Send something before you call. Do your homework about the prospect's company and the likely need for your offering, and work that into your opening (be careful to do this very lightly so you can get to your point).

- If you get a rejection, and the tone is friendly, ask if you could call again to see if things have changed at a certain time in the future, perhaps three or six months. You've moved your "temperature" from cold to at least lukewarm on your next try.

Cold-calling really is an art and it takes time to get over your fears. Hopefully, these techniques and suggestions will guide you on your way to success.

The Sales Call Process
You Can't Live (or Sell) Without

Before you get creative, master the fundamental techniques here first.

SUPPOSE YOU HAVE a phone list with a dozen prospects to call today. How do you structure each conversation? The key is to approach the conversation as a problem-solving discussion, positioning your offering as the solution. The techniques below can apply equally to a face-to-face meeting.

Preparing

Prepare yourself: Be sure you really know your products or services, and have a quick way of describing your company (it's sometimes called an elevator speech). Look up your prospect on the Internet or elsewhere and find out about potential pain points that match your offering. Prepare responses to objections and practice them out loud. If you feel nervous or draggy, get out of your chair and walk around before the phone call, because "motion makes emotion." Do what you need to do so you feel prepared; then you can sound and feel confident and friendly.

Introducing yourself

Make a good first impression. Capture your prospect's attention right out of the gate by introducing yourself and explaining the purpose for your call. Do your best not to sound like a robot, and speak clearly. Establish your own personality on the phone and make your script your own. Project warmth, enthusiasm and energy in your voice! It may be possible to do something to lighten the tone, but be professional above all.

Questioning

If your prospect remains open to talking or agrees to set a time to talk further, you're doing fine. When you continue, give more brief, concise information that will help the prospect understand why you called. Set the stage for naming the problems your offering can help solve. Assist and enable, rather than assume, sell or push. Try to answer questions without debating. Here's where your prepared rebuttals will prove helpful. For any questions you didn't anticipate, don't bluff if you don't have an answer. Promise to come back with one and do so before your own deadline.

Listening and interpreting

Actively listen to the prospect's needs, problems and requirements and keep your answers brief so you don't lose her attention. Your goal should be that your prospect is doing about 80 percent of the talking. In some selling situations, you might be able to read how it's going well enough to close the deal in your first contact. In others, your goal is a second conversation, permission to send more information or samples, a presentation, a meeting, etc.

Informing and educating

Overall, don't try to "sell" her. Let her sell herself; demonstrate how using your product or service would be a great business decision and problem-solver. People typically don't appreciate a pushy salesperson.

Involving and coordinating

Let her know that the delivery process will be smooth, and that you'll walk her through things and be available throughout. Also, that if she has any questions, you'll be there to guide her. People like to be reassured—it's like having a guarantee on a product's box. Make sure you follow through on your commitments here, as failing to do so will harm your credibility and the possibility of repeat business.

Keeping in touch and restarting the cycle

After delivery, show your new customer your professionalism with a simple follow-up call. Let her know that you value her business and you haven't forgotten about her. Make sure the delivery process went well and listen for ways to improve it next time. Confirm that all of her needs were met; answer questions or concerns that she may have regarding the sale or the payment process. And ask when you should be back in touch for the next sales cycle!

CHAPTER IV

How to Keep Customers

Perception is Reality

*What your customers think and feel matters. Ignore
perceptions at your peril!*

AS YOU BUILD a new business, you work to meet or exceed customer expectations. Understanding what customers and prospects are looking for and anticipating their expectations is a proven building block for success. But there's a shadowy aspect of customers' thinking: A lot has to do with the elusive world of market perceptions.

You might think you can get on top of perceptions by collecting data and analyzing results, trends and profiles to understand what has happened historically. No doubt, that exercise will give you important information you can act on. The challenge is that past behavior does not necessarily dictate future actions. The effect of *perception* on behavior is underestimated and is often less visible. People often defy all logic, facts and reason to act based on their perceptions.

Some obvious examples that occur every day include:

- Stock market fluctuations, due to news stories or world events, that inflate or deflate affected companies' share values

- The sudden surge in sales of a product due to sensational media coverage or a viral marketing success

- Consumers who lose confidence in a given product because of negative publicity about a related but different one

The important point about perception is recognizing that people may make decisions regardless of the actual facts. All the effort in the world to explain and prove facts that are clearly evident may not change someone's perception. Still, to ignore these perceptions is dangerous.

What can you do? Look for opportunities to ask current customers, one on one, how they currently perceive your company and offerings. Select some key customers and ask for their guidance for improving perceptions of your company. Listen and avoid becoming defensive, and if you act on their input, let them know you appreciate their directing your attention to an issue. Tell them what you've done about it when you've completed your response.

If you can, consider holding periodic customer appreciation events during which you do of course show appreciation—but also structure the events to provide a forum for feedback, free advice, constructive criticism and so forth for you. A good format for this is a breakfast or lunch with an interesting speaker, followed by a facilitated discussion of the speaker's ideas. You can then gather customer perceptions via a separate section of the program or via surveys you provide during the event. Take care when you combine a bunch of customers and prospects in this regard, as discussions can occasionally get out of hand. For this reason, some entrepreneurs choose only to follow the one-on-one route.

Of course, your prospects and customers have full agendas, and it's not their job to constantly coach you. But strategically timed, occasional contacts like these will give you a good barometer of customer perceptions—and a lot to think about.

It's not always easy to keep an open mind when it comes to prospects' and customers' perception of your product or service. While something may be perceived one way by its creators or distributors, what really matters is how it's perceived by the market. The key is to recognize and accept the presence of perception and manage programs and business initiatives to respond to perception as part of your ongoing business.

Understanding and Adjusting to Consumer Behavior Changes

Don't let your customers' behavior surprise you.
There's a method to their madness.

CONSUMER BEHAVIOR REFERS to people's selection, purchase and consumption of goods and services to satisfy of their needs and desires.

A number of factors influence consumer behavior. They include cultural, social and economic factors. Here are a few.

Culture is the part of a particular society that guides the behavior of people in it. Different cultures exhibit different consumer behavior. Some cultures only trade in cash; some are strictly vegetarian. If your company does business outside of the culture(s) with which you are really familiar, make sure you understand the impact of those cultures on your business there.

Social class also influences consumer behavior. Various factors can get mixed into social class impacts, e.g., income level, family role, education or work. Members of the same social class tend to have the same consumer behavior. Drilling further down, different members of a family may be responsible for different buying decisions. If the buying decision for televisions is made by the husband, marketers should opt for advertisement strategies that appeal to men.

Social groups form around social roles such as work life, political party, gender or hobby. Members of some social groups all share a single attitude toward certain products; hence their consumer behavior will be similar. But other social groups don't exhibit unified views or preferences. So if your business targets social groups, you need to know how uniform their preferences are and market accordingly.

Consumers play different roles at the same time, considering their social groups, roles in an extended family, and any organizations they join. For example, a teacher may be a political party member, a bird-watcher, a parent and the son of an aging couple as well. Each of his roles influences his buying behavior.

Personal factors such as lifestyle, occupation, age and personality also influence consumer behavior. For instance, as people age, their purchase behavior of goods and services keeps changing. Your company may market a product that keeps a customer for decades (think life insurance) or keeps focused on an evergreen group (there are always new three-year-olds).

Occupation also influences consumer behavior. A business professional may have to buy suits for work; a blue-collar laborer may buy casual clothes. Often, a job dictates one's after-work lifestyle, which also affects buying behavior.

Psychological factors are yet another element which influences consumer behavior. Consumer confidence, the broad perception in a large group about how a country's economy is doing, can especially affect major purchases and savings rates. At the individual level, a person's motivation to buy something can range from a pressing need to sheer impulse.

Of course, if marketing teams could crack the mysteries of consumer behavior, life would be quite different. The point is to make informed decisions based on the best understanding you have of your customer, keep monitoring how well you are connecting, and update or change your marketing when you see changes in behavior.

In all this activity, let's not underestimate the importance of marketing via the Internet. With a simple connection to the worldwide web, the Internet can be used in countless ways. One advantage it offers is a much quicker time-frame for marketing changes. If you need to redesign a physical product display, you can expect days or weeks to go by before it's on the shop floors. If you want to change a web marketing page, or re-price something in your online store, it can be done in a matter of minutes. Marketers must take advantage of websites, blogs and social media channels to constantly promote their goods to consumers. The virtual world connects marketers with new and different consumers, too. Simply put, a changing society leads to people being choosy and wanting choices at all times.

Knowing these critical fundamentals, a top marketer or sales professional should be able to:

- Build good relationships and get input from customers to guide sales and marketing messages and techniques.

- Give customers time to express feedback—good or bad.

- Understand their customer base, and then help them with their buying needs.

- Create a good rapport and make it easy for the customer to stay loyal.

These components embody a good strategy of dealing with any shift in consumer behavior in the market. Applying these principles while constantly listening to consumers' needs is the path to success.

Keeping Customers for Life

Like a friendship, your relationship with your
customers should be built on trust and confidence.

GOOD SERVICE to customers can distinguish you from competitors. But giving good service can also help keep customers for life. To build a long-term relationship with them, you must know their goals, identify what they need, and provide solutions to those needs.

In order to keep customers for life, demonstrate to customers and prospects that your services and products are as right for you as they are for them. For instance, if you sell Honda cars and drive a Honda yourself, prospects are more likely to believe that you must actually think it's a good car.

When customers buy from you for the first time, the relationship has only just begun. It is now your responsibility to make sure that this relationship thrives, by communicating with them and checking to see if they need more products or services from you. This will show them that you are concerned about their needs and desires, and that can keep them coming back to you for life.

To support long-term relationships with customers, it helps to show them that you have their best interests at heart. Demonstrate that you are someone they can trust. You never know—they might refer other customers to you if you are good at maintaining a long-term business relationship.

Rewarding your customers goes a long way in keeping customers for life. Send them gifts in the form of coupons, discounts or other exclusive benefits. Many businesspeople don't return phone calls, so if you ensure that you do, and promptly, it will earn you points with your customers. Don't make empty promises to your customers, and if you do make promises, make sure you deliver on them. If you say a product will be delivered on a certain day, and a problem arises, tell them as soon as you learn of a delay. Most people would rather hear bad news right away, because it gives them a chance to respond. They don't appreciate being the last to hear about a problem that's been brewing for some time.

Try always to be easily accessible in case of a problem with a customer. This will show your customers that your business is open for their interests, and not yours. Make especially sure that new customers perceive this about you and see you as a business owner who puts their needs first. Doing this consistently will keep customers coming back and saying good things about your company to others.

Maintain communication with your customers through emails, texts or phone calls. Do all you can to deepen and broaden your relationship with them. A solid bond in business is a rare and extremely valuable asset these days.

Customer Loyalty Programs

*Your business depends on them. Make sure you're
treating them right with these proven tips.*

BUILDING A CUSTOMER LOYALTY PROGRAM can be an important tool
for the success of your business. It helps ensure that you attract new customers
and retain old ones as well. Competition is becoming stiffer all the time, so you
need to be armed with a number of strategies to keep your customers coming
back for more.

Keeping track of your customers is important if you want to create a good
customer loyalty program. Use software to remind yourself of key dates in their business and perhaps their private lives and send a personal greeting when those dates roll
around. If your business has a huge customer base, look into an automated greeting.
You'll be surprised at how many customers will reply with thanks for your thought-
fulness, giving you an opportunity to ask if there's anything you can do for them now.

Regarding your choice of loyalty program options, why not ask some or all
of your customers what they prefer? You can slip in a few other survey questions
as well, if you want other input. By doing this, you show their views matter. And
the results will help you identify things you can improve and rule out programs
that will have little impact or a negative results.

Keep visible in other ways too. Some customers may need reminders that
your business exists. You can do this by sending emails or letters with info, news,
promotions and discounts. Ensure that the rewards you are giving your customers are easily obtained. Rewards generate good will and interest in your program.

If your business is not suited to coupons and other promotions, consider
revising your pricing schedules to encourage bulk, regular or repeat orders. It's not
a typical loyalty program, but you can announce it as one and even make it available only to customers who have given you a certain level of business in the past.
Others can qualify by buying lots more!

Selling gift cards that can be used to buy your products and services can also build customer loyalty, especially if you sell them at a discount off their face value. People love coupons and discounts, so you're giving them something they really appreciate. And although you aren't doing a gift card program to add extra profit, you probably will gain at least some extra profit from your gift cards. Studies show that a surprising number of them are never redeemed, meaning you have made a sale (the card) that has virtually no cost of goods attached.

Communication is a key factor in establishing a loyalty program with your customers. It enables you to communicate with your current customers instead of having to wait for them to come and purchase something. Customers who are told about the loyalty program will be pleased to know that your company has actually taken the initiative to recognize them as being part of your company's success.

How to Communicate Effectively with Customers

Communication with customers is more than a
monetary transaction. Learn some great tips here.

AS YOUR BUSINESS continues to grow, getting new customers becomes less difficult. However, sometimes communicating with both old and new customers can be difficult, even though communicating with longer-standing customers is typically easier than trying to get new ones.

If you do not keep in touch with your customers, you will not be able to maintain the long-term relationship that is a main factor that leads to many successes in business. You need occasions to learn what's new for them and to express your own ideas, opinions, advice and strategies—preferably in person. You may feel like spending time with them is a waste, but it very often leads to expanded business, thanks to your knowledge of what your customers want and expect from you.

Here are some tips that will help you communicate effectively with your customers and build a long-lasting relationship.

- If your customers ask to speak with you about an issue, suggest that you meet in person, if possible. Most people appreciate the accommodation of face-to-face conversation. If that is not possible, consider a webcam call. Note your customers' facial expressions when making your points. Be clear on your key message and ensure sensitivity to the schedule of your customer.

- Before you meet or have a call, list your objectives and the key points of discussion. Ensure that each point has been discussed and ironed out thoroughly as you go through the meeting. Note any concerns your customer brings up, and make sure you address them, either in your meeting or later.

- Communicating can be hard work, especially if you have a large portfolio of customers. Therefore, it is good to have a system to record what was discussed with whom, to avoid forgetting key points that were raised by your customer that might be very important to them. You can do this by keeping folders in your email account for each customer, or by making files on your computer hard drive.

- You should always present neat, professional-looking materials to customers, e.g., contracts, manuals, brochures, etc. Ensure you have the correct information listed in the brochures and that contracts are well-written with proper addresses and monetary amounts, so that there isn't a misunderstanding about any of the terms and conditions.

- Don't be afraid to advise your customers about a product or service they need, despite the fact that they might seem to know exactly what they want.

- With your particular set of skills and expertise in the industry, you also should be able to explain to them why a given product is not a good match for them. This improves your credibility, since it shows your customers that you are not out there just to collect money from them. You are clearly looking out for their best interests. Ensure, though, that if you suggest an alternate product for them, you do it without sounding forceful. If they still want their original product, agree with their request, and give them an open invitation to call or stop by if they have any problems.

These customer meetings can often open up new ways of working together with your long-standing customers. It can be fun, and it certainly can be rewarding.

CHAPTER V
Branding

Branding Your Business

Your business's brand is its personality.
Be sure it's vibrant.

YOUR BRAND can be a significant asset, given today's fierce competition. It is an essential element of the marketing strategy for any business, big or small. But before we think about the branding process, we should first understand what we mean by a brand.

A brand is the market identity of a product, service or business. It can take many forms, including a name, sign, symbol, color combination, sound, or slogan. It marks the commercial individuality of a given business, and should evoke the values or other key characteristics of a business and its owners. A brand speaks about your offering and how you and it are different from your competitors. So it's worth investing serious thought to create and build a unique and fitting brand. Think of your brand as your business's face and personality. It starts a dialog with buyers as they decide whether to do business with you or with your competitors.

Experts are there with advice on how to create an effective brand for the products and services of an organization. It's smart to conduct research to ensure that the name you prefer isn't already taken by someone else in the marketplace. There is more than a legal reason for this; if you have a plan for major expansion, you don't want your customers to confuse your company with another one in your industry. In short, your brand name should be unique for a multitude of reasons.

It helps to think of a hierarchy that describes your brand and other similar marketing elements. Your overall brand sits at the top. Your company name, logo, tagline and so forth are under it. Depending on the complexity of your business, you may then have one or more product or service brands, perhaps for groups of offerings. They will carry your logo and their own brand. They will probably have *brand names*, but those are not the same as the overall brand.

In effect, your brand is a promise. It is a commitment to customers that you will deliver on your offering in keeping with your values. Effective brands promote your success in many ways:

- They help in market segmentation by distinguishing your product or service from others traded in your market.

- They create a memorable personality for your product or organization.

- They develop trust among buyers. If the buyer has a good experience with a purchase under your brand, that positive feeling can transfer to another of your offerings.

- Over time, branding can develop what's called brand loyalty among your customers and squeeze out the competition. Ideally, the next time a former customer has a need, they'll check your website or the store shelf to see if you offer something they can use for their need.

The brand development process

You may already have a brand, or you may be ready to develop one. If you already have one, give it a long, hard look, including asking for input from a variety of contacts. Does it work well for you? Sometimes start-ups just throw something together so they can print business cards and get rolling. It's perfectly fine to change to a more sophisticated, harder working brand later, if your first stab was not a success. Just don't do it very often. If your current brand has fairly good recognition in your market but you're not satisfied with it, it may pay to try to develop a new brand that somehow links back to your original one.

Start your process by thinking carefully about what you want to express through your brand. Accuracy? Reliability? Fun? Trendiness? Draw up a list and prioritize your ideas. You won't be able to capture all of them in your branding, but they will form a cluster that should point to your unique market identity. And they will give you a reason to weed out bad designs and strategies, ones that just don't fit with your brand.

Also, do some basic market research in order to garner impressions regarding brand names. For instance, summon several focus groups to gather their responses to a range of names; these can be friends or family members, too. In fact—true story—my mother-in-law thought up the name of this book series during just such an informal focus group! Formulate a way that customers can provide various potential names for you. One way to do this is through the use of survey cards.

Of course, you also need a logo. Your company name, logo icon and tag line constitute your total logo design. General Electric's curly GE in a circle, and the tagline "We bring good things to life," is one successful total logo design.

Because branding is important, it's worth investing money to ensure you're getting the best possible design work. Shop around for a good logo designer and in addition to reviewing the portfolio, get references from customers. Studies have shown that different colors promote different emotions, so ensure the colors you select convey your company's personality correctly.

The best branding work conveys the values of the company, plans of growth, vision, and mission. They say your brand is want you *want* customers to perceive, and what they perceive is your *image*. The challenge is to make them match.

When your branding devices are final, you will need to protect them legally as intellectual property with trademark or copyright registrations. The difference between a trademark and a copyright is important.

- A trademark protects words, phrases and logos used to identify the source of goods and services.

- A copyright protects works of authorship as fixed in a tangible form of expression.

Keep in mind that there may be occasions when both copyright and trademark protection is needed for the same project. For example, a marketing campaign for a new product may introduce a new slogan for use with the product, which also appears in advertisements for the product. The advertisement's text and graphics, as published, will be covered by copyright. This will not, however, protect the slogan. The slogan may be protected by trademark law, but this will not cover the rest of the advertisement. If you want both forms of protection, you will have to perform both types of registration with your government's appropriate offices. The Internet will lead you to the right contacts in governmental offices handling trademark and copyright issues.

Branding and Mnemonics

How do you get people to remember you exist?

THE USE OF MNEMONICS is a great way to enhance your brand awareness and recognition. A mnemonic is a memory device that help people recall larger pieces of information through short verbal and non-verbal connections.

There are many kinds of mnemonics. The most important ones are music, model and word (or expression) mnemonics. If you are interested in this kind of branding tool, make sure you have the list of attributes you want to reinforce that you drew up earlier handy. The whole point is to underscore them in the mind of the beholder.

With that in mind, be sure to test whatever you think would work on a wide variety of potential users of your offering. Get them to tell you what attributes your picks suggest to them. This is a highly subjective business, but generally you'll find a consensus emerges if you test your front-runners on a wide enough sampling. Here are some examples of mnemonics at work.

- *Musical Mnemonics* come in many different forms, such as jingles, poems, songs or musical chimes. Think of Microsoft Window's opening and closing notes, the Intel chime, and others. When you hear those sounds, you instantly think of their owners.

- *Model Mnemonics* include logos, images, signs and mascots. Ronald McDonald of McDonalds and all the team mascots you can think of are good examples. As soon as you see these mascots in the media, you automatically think of their owners.

- *Word or Expression Mnemonics* include short phrases that convey the key attributes of their owners. Taglines are one form of these aids. They may be changed more frequently than things like logos, reflecting new marketing initiatives, but they still should support your brand. Apple's "Think Different" is a good example, as its unconventional grammar suggests out-of-the-box solutions.

Whether your branding exercise is modest or extensive (read expensive), it's really worth doing. Your branding should never stop evolving; it should grow along with your business.

Launching and Sustaining Your Brand

It's not a one-time event, but a continuous process.

IF YOU ALREADY ARE an entrepreneur, you know what it's like to brainstorm an idea, turn it into a fully-developed plan, and then start executing it to create a small business. This process is often an incredibly rewarding experience, all the more so if you achieve some success. Even if your ideas are not groundbreaking or your products or services are not necessarily original or unique, it's still *your* company. When you see your company's name on your business card, building or product, you feel a sense of pride. Your reputation is on the line, for the world to see, represented by your brand.

Launching and building your brand

Let's first assume you are still in the planning stages and need to create a brand. What is it all about?

A brand is more than a tag line or slogan. It's an expressive bridge, supporting the relationship your company shares with your customers and the rest of the world. Keeping in front of their eyes, encouraging those customers to keep coming back and also having them tell others helps build your brand. Launching a brand can be simple or complicated, depending on the scale that's appropriate for your business and budget, but either way, it does require your focused attention. Identifying some key components of launching and building a brand is essential for success.

Research: If you haven't done your homework yet, it's time to start. First define the environment in which your company will operate. *Who are the leaders among your competitors? What made them successful? What made less successful ones fail? Which companies created flourishing brand awareness or strength and how did they do it? What messages do the leaders send in their branding?* Searching the Internet for helpful history, interviewing successful business owners, identifying the pitfalls that could be looming, and understanding the market in which your brand will operate will help you understand how to position your brand and company.

Master your market: After your initial research, consider how you want to attack the market in which you will operate. Begin by finding out how the competition operates. *What are local consumers saying about the market itself? How loyal is the typical customer of the major players in your market? How do these players attract and hold customers? What is the main selling point of each of your competitors? Is there a common theme among these selling points?* Knowing how your competition goes to market will help you establish your brand with confidence. Even if your brand will be based on straightforward standards such as quick delivery, 100 percent reliability, excellent customer service or the lowest pricing, you will know it's driven by the needs or wants of the customers you are after.

Get plugged in: When your initial branding materials are ready, introduce your new business to the community. Make sure prominent individuals, media influencers, other business owners, and even local chamber of commerce and government officials know who you are and what you do. This not only includes providing these entities with information about your new business, it's an opportunity to share your mission, values and goals, and to increase your brand strength with them. A confident owner with a well-thought out brand campaign can make significant inroads in the local community, taking advantage of press releases, newsletters, open house days, trade shows, professional organizations, word-of-mouth chatter and solid business-to-business (B2B) referrals.

Sustaining your brand

Once you have launched your business successfully and others know about your presence in the market, you will be well on your way to new growth and expansion. The next phase is all about growing and supporting your brand. For great results, here's some proven advice.

Don't get complacent: Staying relevant is a must. Even if your launch is successful, after a period of time your brand could still suffer by not attracting new customers, keeping established customers loyal, and continuing the flow of referrals. Try spreading your brand awareness to new audiences within your market—this can return immense results. Examine the demographics of your current customer base and ask if there are new ways to reach them. Where do they go? How do they find out about products or services like yours, and are you there? What other businesses or contact networks that you haven't reached out to could possibly help spread your brand messaging to others? Staying relevant is vital; but becoming the market leader is the goal.

Hire the pros: If the growth of your company or scale of your business permits, consider working with one of the professional companies in the branding business. They can be one of the most vital outsource organizations you could hire. You may have not had the funds to go this route as you launched. But now that your business is has a track record of success, a solid branding outfit can take you to a level not possible before. These professionals can review your current messaging, marketing materials, website layout, product packaging, collateral pieces (brochures, etc.) and other important components and make critical evaluations. Those evaluations can then help you turn your branding into a synergistic approach across all types of media. Suddenly your brand has a complete, integrated identity with accompanying messaging. This tightly targeted attack now captures everyone at the same time with the same broad communication points about your business and its mission.

Review and revise accordingly: Down the road, the market may change. You'll have to be ready to respond if it does. Factors such as new competition or technology, the overall economy, customers' wants and needs, government decisions and other aspects of the external business environment may dictate this action. Your customer base could also change habits or situations. Plan to review and if necessary, revise your brand messaging and positions periodically. You will find that either nothing major needs to be done beyond a few small tweaks, or it may be time to change and update your brand to not only stay relevant, but to maintain current market leadership. Identifying, understanding and attacking branding challenges successfully will give your small business the best odds of success.

CHAPTER VI

Tricks of the Trade

Effective Networking through Social Media Channels

Facebook has 680 million members worldwide.
How many people heard about your business today?

UNDERSTANDING SOCIAL MEDIA and how to use them improves your success rates in virtual networking initiatives. Understanding the various types of social media channels that are available will shorten that process.

Before we begin, it's important to understand that networking is directly related to sales success. Sales directly link the visibility and popularity of the seller with the desire of the buyer, and both visibility and popularity are directly linked to networking. It's generally true that the more people know about your business or offerings, the more people will be interested in them. Social media offers a way for your business to become known to a lot of people without much effort. It's all in how you use it. As we've previously discussed about the Law of Large Numbers, the larger the group of people who know about your business, the better your odds are that some will ultimately become customers.

Social media use web-based and mobile technologies to turn communication into interactive dialogue (media for social interaction). Although most people plugging in and logging-on these days use some form of social media, many of them use it for fun or leisure activities.

In today's ultra-competitive struggle to capture the consumer's attention, a social media initiative can be an effective, inexpensive way to touch "unreachable" buyers, those overlooked by traditional methods. Many different types of social media channels can be used to support effective networking. Let's take a look at a few.

Social networking channels offer excellent platforms through which you can build good networks. These channels provide features such as public or private messaging, instant messaging services, upload capabilities for photos and videos, and functions to help you form special interest groups. Often, you can make event announcements and display your personal contact information for others. These types of channels deliver widespread appeal to many people or particular groups sharing demographic characteristics with you. Examples of social networking channels that have revolutionized communication around the world during recent times include ASmallWorld, Bebo, Cyworld, Diaspora, eHarmony, Facebook, Friendster, Hi5, Hyves, LinkedIn, Match.com, MySpace, Ning, Orkut, Plaxo, Tagged, XING and IRC.

Blogging is another social media channel. It's widely used and has gained importance for people interested in creating online networks related to their work or cause. Blogging provides the opportunity to write an idea or a well-argued comment on certain issues and then post them to a blog space. Interesting and engaging blogs attract comments and reactions from readers, who may invite others to your blog site or simply forward your online location to their colleagues and friends. This can significantly increase your online traffic and readership, as your message provokes others to stay involved and stay tuned. Hot blogging sites include Blogger, Blogspot, ExpressionEngine, LiveJournal, Open Diary, TypePad, Vox, WordPress and Xanga.

Micro blogging is worth considering if you are serious about forming a good online community. An excellent of example of such a channel is Twitter, which not only offers blogging capabilities, but also provides an excellent opportunity through which users can create links and use the connections to create a following. Micro blogging is usually brief messaging with multiple updates, often within the same day. Popular micro blogging sites are FMyLife, Foursquare, Jaiku, Plurk, Posterous, Tumblr, Twitter, Qaiku, Yammer and Google Buzz.

Social bookmarking is gaining in importance and could perhaps be the missing link to having an expansive network (social news and social tagging can be included here, too). Social bookmarking works in a simple way. Blog posts and updates are stored in an online directory, such as CiteULike, Delicious, Diigo, Google Reader, StumbleUpon, folkd, Digg, Mixx, NowPublic, Reddit and Newsvine. They can even be searched by a search engine seeking posts containing certain words. Such facilities are also used to direct traffic to your blog site. In this way, it becomes possible to draw subtantial online traffic to your blog or updates over time.

Internet forums (or discussion forums) remain important tools for creating online networks. They have in been in use for quite some time. By responding to, or *mediating* over multiple commentators' positions or opinions regarding a certain issue or topic, it is possible to create a large network of active users. (The *Mediator* of an Internet forum controls the content of the forum. He deletes off-topic or offensive posts, or guides the discussion in one direction or another.) Discussion forums are also very good tools for entrepreneurs, in that they provide a unique kind of feedback. This is especially valuable to businesses that depend on consumer feedback to develop or update certain products.

Email marketing and *video marketing* are self-explanatory. They have gained mass appeal in the virtual world. When implemented properly, these channels can be easily maximized to generate significant traffic. For example, it is possible to have attachments with an email message. Consider the addition of attractive graphics, video, or an audio message to complement your messages as well. By enhancing your message in these ways, the communication becomes more engaging than a plain email message. These formats can include Google Docs, Docs.com, Dropbox.com, Flickr, Viddler, Vimeo, YouTube and Ustream.

Another way of increasing effectiveness in the use of social media channels is using a combination of channels. Then you can leverage the advantages offered by each, while effectively overcoming their limitations. Eventually, through integration, it becomes possible to direct more traffic to your chosen social media channels and thus build a good network.

When using a social networking medium such as Facebook, enrich the experience for others by uploading graphics, video or audio files to produce a more interactive form of communication. Similarly, you can include links to your social networking sites at the bottom of an email address or other marketing collaterals, such as brochures or business cards. Carefully balancing these channels will give you the kind of network you want.

Avoiding Sales Burnout

It's called "The Demon" for a reason. Being able to identify it and knowing how to defeat it is particularly important in a start-up's early days.

BURNOUT—WE'VE ALL HEARD about it. Many have experienced it. Everybody tries to avoid it. Most don't understand it or see it coming. The feelings of stress, irritability, indecision, lack of concern for your work, exhaustion or fatigue can be debilitating for anyone in business, but perhaps it's even worse for entrepreneurs.

One definition for burnout is "exhaustion of physical or emotional strength or motivation, usually as a result of prolonged stress or frustration." It starts with disproportionate and protracted levels of stress. The tension you feel leaves you unable to cope with tasks or projects. With time the tension progresses to apathy, boredom and lackluster performance.

Sales burnout affects entrepreneurs who are doing their own selling, as well as those who manage salespeople, not to mention the salespeople they manage. The brand new start-up entrepreneur, worn out from doing a hundred other things, is more likely to succumb to sales burnout because his sales hat is only one of many he wears. And he knows that this critical period is when he really must dig in and sell-sell-sell to get his new business off the ground.

At exactly the moment when sales may mean survival or failure, you can get caught up in burnout and succumb to one of the worst pitfalls you can imagine. If your salespeople share your sense of urgency too intensely, they can share your burnout too! That's why it is so important to learn to recognize and avoid sales burnout.

Burnout has many causes. Some are external, like bad health, family concerns, or other personal stress. But often, it can be due to the job itself: stringent work schedules, unrealistic quotas, excessive travel, problems with production or delivery, non-paying customers, etc. Burnout can also be a result of the work environment (poor working conditions, inadequate infrastructure, a ton of boring but necessary daily tasks, friction among partners or co-workers, poor hires who don't pull their weight).

Identifying the causes and indicators of burnout and taking action to combat it can possibly save your company's and your own life. Dealing with it can be instrumental in maintaining your sanity, keeping the peace at home, and making you a more productive entrepreneur.

Burnout doesn't happen all at once. It usually has a slow, snowballing effect, despite modest warning signs along the way. If left unattended, it can progress into intense symptoms, such as nausea at the mere thought of going to work each day. However, there are some things you can do to delay or prevent burnout from sneaking into your work life and the lives of your teammates. Here are a few simple suggestions. Use them on yourself if necessary, or coach your colleagues if you are concerned that they are heading down the burnout path.

- **Leave your work *at* your workplace.** When the clock indicates the official work day is done (regardless whether your projects or all your daily to-do items are complete), head for home. You may not be able to pull this off every day, but doing so once or twice a week makes a huge difference.

- **Set a cut-off time for all electronic devices.** Most of us are practically incapable of turning off our smart phones during the day, and many of us have trouble doing it even after we get home for the night. Try setting a time to turn off phones, laptops and tablets, even for recreation. It will give you back nourishing personal time with family, friends, a good book or favorite television show.

- **Stay in shape and take care of yourself.** The last thing you need when quotas, vendors and deadlines are hovering around you like vultures is to be stressed, out-of-shape, undernourished or sleep-deprived. Make time for a proper night's sleep, hit the gym, exercise, and find the time to eat sensibly. You will be amazed at what you can accomplish when you're rested, fueled-up and strong in mind and body.

- **Take a vacation.** You deserve it, just like anyone else, so take advantage of some well-deserved time off when the signs of burnout begin to appear. Even if it's only an afternoon off to see your kid play a key game, a "day-cation" or a long weekend doing things you enjoy, time away from the daily grind is vital for the long haul in business. After all, your career as an entrepreneur is a marathon, not a sprint.

- **Change your routine.** Little changes in your daily tasks, the order in which you do things, or even the route you take to work help refresh you, since moderate changes that *you* instigate are always invigorating. Shake up your day. Change the time you get up in the morning, the time you finish work, and where you go for lunch. A change in routine helps you out of the rut and points to a new way to the finish line.

- **Give yourself the best places to work.** Working from home may make you more productive on some tasks, so exploit this option when possible. But stay attuned to your team's need to see and have access to you. Entrepreneurs sometimes forget how important they are to the rest of their company.

If you try these things and still are suffering, a more aggressive approach may be necessary to beat burnout back. Don't be afraid to reach out to professionals. Psychologists, life coaches, sales coaches, human resource professionals, relaxation experts and religious advisors can be important resources. And don't be a hero: A simple dialogue with colleagues (within or outside your company) and other professionals in your industry may be a source of insight and support in defeating burnout.

The effects of burnout are hard to exaggerate. So watch for it in yourself and in others around you. A start-up is a hotbed for stress, just as it is for reward, so don't underestimate the need for balance and healthy ways.

Outsourcing Your Sales and Marketing

Desperate economic time may call for drastic measures.
Keep sales up by keeping your staff numbers down.
Here's how.

MANY REASONS CAN EXPLAIN why a business would consider outsourcing a sales and marketing team. The main one is to ensure achievement of sales targets at a lower cost. Salaries, benefits, travel, bonuses and so forth add up fast. Some situations that lead to outsourcing are scary, but that's not always so.

Some companies make the decision to outsource to keep from going out of business entirely. If outsourcing sales becomes a survival plan for you, try to retain your key sales team members as long as feasible. They can help you assess and identify areas in which outsourcing can be considered. They also may be able to change roles and manage some of the outsource partner's activities, with the benefit of their grounding in your company. At the same time, it's important to do an internal audit of your weaknesses. You'll want to ensure that your outsource provider does not inherit problems you should first fix yourselves.

Outsourcing saves valuable resources you would otherwise spend on deploying salespeople to new or distant work locations, particularly in other cultures or countries. The right partner abroad can extend your reach and leverage local contacts you would spend years developing yourselves.

Outsourcing certain sales and marketing functions in which your team lacks expertise could be another reason to consider it. For example, brand activations or rebranding activities can be assigned to providers who specialize in these things. Or perhaps your products and services could be sold in an entirely new sales channel. Why re-invent the wheel? Sign up with an appropriate sales force and bank the checks.

As with any major move, do your homework and make sure the transition is fully supported so it has the best chance of succeeding. Over-communicate initially, until you are satisfied the new external team is working productively and smoothly. Make clear whatever reporting and payment expectations you have via written agreements and hold periodic business reviews to monitor progress or intercept problems early.

It's easy to do the same-old same-old just because you haven't had experience with something quite different. So if you haven't worked with outsource vendors, don't automatically rule them out. They could enhance what you're doing today and help you jump faster to the next level.

Mobile Device Marketing: Not Just for Whippersnappers Any More

*Some of the oldest top companies in the world have
the most elaborate mobile marketing campaigns.
Why? Because they want to stay at the top.*

DOES ANYONE ever open a junk mail envelope these days? I don't. I pity the poor entrepreneur who spends all that money from her marketing budget on work, paper, printing, graphic design, lead list fees, and postage, only to have 95 percent of it go right into the trash without it even being opened. Why not just pay for a targeted electronic lead list and an unlimited mobile device calling plan and send a text message (also called an SMS) instead?

Seriously. A few of you old-timers might be chuckling at the thought of phone text marketing. Ready for the punch line?

Text messages have a 95 percent OPEN rate. Now who's chuckling?

Mobile marketing is a set of practices that enables organizations to communicate and engage with their audience in an interactive, relevant manner through any mobile device or network. Specifically, mobile devices can include smart phones, feature phones, and any handheld device capable of surfing the web. While these techniques work best in business-to-consumer (B2C) applications, with creativity, successful business-to-business (B2B) applications can work as well. For instance, texting discount codes applicable to orders placed before a certain deadline has worked well on distributors who usually like to wait until the last minute to order. Also, you can send a customer a coupon via mobile devices. Imagine being able to show a coupon received on your phone to the store clerk. It saves your customer time and money. How many times have you left a coupon in the car or at home? Below are several traits of mobile marketing and why it is the new way to market that entrepreneurs can expect to grow exponentially in the future.

Trait 1: Convenience

A mobile-enabled website makes it easy for customers to browse websites on mobile devices. If your site is not mobile-ready, users will have to pinch, zoom, and scroll their way all over your site.

Trait 2: Geo-Targeted

One in three mobile searches has *local intent*; that is, one out of three searches is made by people searching for the location of a local business. Virtually all new smart phones come with GPS. This is very helpful because customers' phones can send their location information and get directions to a given destination. Nowadays, if I'm using my smart phone to search for a nearby business, if that business doesn't have a link to a GPS app, I just won't do business with it, because so many of its competitors do. It's a perfect example of why you *have* to keep up with technology and the evolution of marketing trends.

Trait 3: Integrated

Successful mobile campaigns tie into the marketing plan of the company. You have to tell people about your company or offerings on as many platforms as possible so that people regularly access it on their smart phones and other mobile devices. By placing the promotion on your website, newsletter, Facebook, LinkedIn, Twitter, Google+, etc., you make it easier for customers to get notifications on their mobile devices.

Trait 4: Timely

You can engage your customer instantly if needed. For example, if you're a hair stylist and someone suddenly cancels an appointment at short notice, you can send out a text to all your clients offering a discount for the first person who replies and agrees to come in at the appointed hour. If you're a restaurant manager and it's a slow Friday night, send a text message offering a special or discount. Your own doctor or dentist may already send you reminder messages about your upcoming appointment—not a bad idea!

Trait 5: Fun

Interacting with users and getting them involved can dramatically increase marketing results. Consider sweepstakes, polls, and contests. If you capture customers' birthdays, send them a special offer along with your congratulations. Tactics like this have all been used successfully to build customer lists and sell products and services.

Trait 6: Exclusive

To encourage people to opt-in to your list, give them a good reason. Present them an exclusive special. An example would be "Text FREE to 12345 for a free cup of coffee."

Trait 7: Not Spam

Successful mobile marketing campaigns ask for permission. They're transparent and also inform the user that additional data or text messaging charges may apply. They must also tell the user how to be removed from the list. Believe me, the last thing you want to do is annoy your message recipients. If you put people off, they will go out of their way to avoid doing business with you. But done well, mobile marketing can really get surprising results.

S.G.

Mastermind Groups:
A Valuable Resource

*Even the brightest minds benefit from exchanging
and testing ideas.*

NEEDLESS TO SAY, NETWORKING has become an important aspect of today's business environment. But for an entrepreneur who is new to the challenges of sales and marketing and looking for a mentor or a sounding board in these areas (and even for an old hand), general networking connections may not be adequate. However, a mastermind group may be just the thing.

So, what is a mastermind group?

A mastermind group or affinity network is a group of individuals who are like-minded and who share similar desires, objectives or goals. The purpose a collection of sales and marketing mastermind group is to keep members on the cutting edge of sales and marketing trends.

In forming such a group, the members agree to share ideas, skills, knowledge, experience, etc. A mastermind group is different from a typical networking circle, in that everyone in a mastermind group is pre-qualified and brings something of value to the table. Networking circles are usually open to the public, while mastermind groups typically admit new members by invitation only.

Here's an example of the kind of thing you might benefit from in your own mastermind group. Salespeople sometimes fail to recognize that buyers can be extremely well informed today. Thanks to the Internet, certain kinds of buyers don't even need salespeople at all. They do their own research and comparative shopping, placing orders for major purchases like cars without even setting foot into a store. This is an important factor that marketers and salespeople must consider. The traditional approach to sales, pegged on striving to *inform* the customer, may not be always relevant these days. A mastermind group may expose you to salespeople and marketeers who have far greater experience than you in these issues. And you, in turn, may have specialized knowledge that others in the group may lack.

So learning about what others have tried—and the results—can shorten your learning curve and steer you away from pitfalls. Of course what may work for one business may not work for another. However the rich range of give and take in a good group's exchanges can help you to judge what may work best for your enterprise.

The dangers of flying solo are obvious, and most entrepreneurs nowadays wouldn't dream of ignoring seasoned or forward-thinking input, even if they later decide it's not for them. Within a mastermind group, the advice, checking questions, support and feedback flow freely. A good one will not let you miss details that are important or get sidetracked by unimportant distractions, since members will always remind you of the goals you've set. You get to return the favor when you can contribute from your own expertise.

How do you get into a Mastermind group? You can start your own with some colleagues you respect. Or you can ask around and surf the web to find groups that sound good and are looking for new members. Going online, you can learn all about these things, including how to run a group session (they can be live, online, via Skype, etc.). Meetup.com, Craigslist and a host of other sites facilitate starting and running groups.

Some entrepreneurs report that joining a mastermind group has made enormous impacts on their businesses. As you probably know, there are failure rates of 95 percent for new businesses in their first couple of months in certain sectors. Thanks to the shared knowledge, candid critiques and encouragement these groups offer, many entrepreneurs say they've been spared from making serious mistakes. And they add that they enjoy the camaraderie, knowledge and connections the group offers. So consider joining a sales and marketing mastermind group and see what it does for you.

Marketing Outside the Box

*In closing, here are a few ways to market your
business that you may not have thought of.*

Market yourself! It all starts with you—advertise your own business. Wear clothes, drive a car, or use other products with your company name and logo on them. Have a laptop bag or protective cover specially printed with your company logo. Talk about your company as much as possible. When people ask what you do for a living, have an elevator speech (lasting no more than a minute) ready. Never leave home without your business cards. Daily life is an open door to advertise your business.

Try co-op marketing. Pay local business owners with similar target markets but noncompetitive offerings a fee to place handouts, flyers, or a poster promoting your product or service in their store or office. Ad swapping also works well.

Consider bus stop ads. Purchase a bus stop advertisement near your business. Follow billboard creation guidelines and keep the text minimal. If the primary audience is foot traffic, you may be able to get away with a lengthier version. Negotiate an ad space with one or more of the local transportation companies with something along the lines of "Take a picture of this bus stop ad, and bring it in for a free widget or X percent off your next purchase or bill."

Ask for referrals. Start up a referral program. I knew a limousine company that gives you a 20 percent referral fee if you bring in an order. Imagine: If you help them book an $800 limousine ride, they give you $160 as a referral fee—who wouldn't do that? That may sound like the company is paying out a lot, but it's better to have 80 percent of something, than 100 percent of nothing. This is a great way to generate new business.

Try aerial advertising. Have a plane or hot air balloon fly above your city with an ad for your product or service. You see them all the time around beaches and events that draw large numbers of people.

Consider bandit signs. Bandit signs are forms of advertising that cost less than a cup of coffee per sign, even cheaper in bulk orders. They are custom-made signs that people place in high-traffic areas. They get their name because they are placed in areas where they will eventually be removed by the city. The idea behind them is simple; it's to generate leads before they are taken down. It may not be the most ethical advertising option, but if you watch out for them, you'll see they are frequently used. People do get bored at intersections, and if you're like me, you'll look at those signs. As a caution, you might contact a few companies who advertise like this and ask if they get fined!

Give bathroom stalls a chance. This one might sound funny, but it has a high probability of making someone read your ad. Advertise on flyers in bathroom stalls of local businesses or public facilities. Think about it! When using the restroom, people just stand or sit there and stare at a (usually) blank wall for at least 30 seconds. Honestly, where else does someone have your undivided attention for *at least* 30 seconds? Talk about a captive audience!

Could a billboard work? Purchase a billboard in a location near your business or on a busy stretch of road. Make a short, clear offer. Less is more with billboards. If you find yourself wishing you had just a bit more space, you've said too much.

Tie in with public events. Get a list of community events in your town and highlight the ones you believe your target market will be attending. Think up any creative ways you could tie your business into the event. If you own a restaurant, you could offer to provide an appetizer for each table. In return, you negotiate with the event to let you include a small flyer which gives the name of the dish, your restaurant's name and any other relevant information—any happy hour deals or half-off appetizers at the designated times—to expand your customer base.

A variation on this theme is to become a sponsor of an event that attracts prospects you want to reach. Usually sponsors get to place an ad in the program, or locate a billboard or flag on the playing field. It gives you nice exposure, and it can generate good will for your company.

Encourage employees to advertise. Incentivize employees to place advertisements on their vehicle, generate fresh leads, or otherwise help to promote your business's growth. Incentivize them with paid time off or anything with a monetary value, such as gift cards, a percentage of the closed sale amount, or, well, money.

Use flyers. Print and post them on bulletin boards around town. Have a few with you in your car at all times in case you find a new bulletin board you can post one on. Also, you can place them on vehicles in the area surrounding your business.

Give a kiosk a try. Set up a kiosk in local shopping malls or high-traffic outdoor areas. Make it moveable so that once you saturate that location, you can move it to a new one and tackle a new market.

Check local ad resources. Advertise in community directories, recreation guides, newsletters sent out by other local businesses, and other local publications in your community.

Test direct marketing. Send a mailer to local homes or businesses. Try to create something unique and different from the other handful of mailers the recipients will receive that week. For small areas, you can hire school kids to drop them off.

Think about buses and taxis. Unfortunately, there's a good and bad side to this idea. Yes, you'll reach a broad audience. But because a lot of the people who see your advertisement may be very far from your place of business, or far from home themselves, they may not act. You'll know if it might work for you. Include your phone and Internet details to make follow-ups easy.

Try pre-movie ads. Local theaters often show advertisements prior to the previews. Believe it or not, they can work—people can't help but look at the giant screen sitting in front of them.

Explore the radio. Advertise on your local radio station. Consider ads that don't sound like ads. A lot of businesses get involved in contests the radio is running, or they have the radio station broadcast live from their business, have the hosts recommend their product, or ask to be interviewed on the air. There are dozens of creative advertising options with radio stations that don't sound like ads. And if you have a non-profit radio station, see if sponsoring a day's broadcasting will let you prepare a non-ad-sounding ad.

Exhibit at a trade show. Network with the decision makers in your industry by exhibiting your product or service at a trade show. If your market is the general public, there are public trade shows and community events at which you can purchase booths, too.

Check out restaurant placemats. Local restaurants sometimes offer advertising space on their menu or placemats. Try to align your target market's favorite restaurants with your ad placements.

Investigate television ads. TV advertising on the big networks can be expensive, but there are a lot of cheaper alternatives, like spots available on local stations or what are called *narrow-cast* stations, like the cooking or sports stations.

If your town has a channel that lists what's on, or a public access network, it's generally pretty affordable to get some TV ads there. If possible, try to make your ad somewhat humorous rather than serious (e.g., Super Bowl commercials). They're a lot more memorable and if you're like me, you will tell everyone about that funny commercial you saw last night. Guess what—mission accomplished; word of mouth advertising is the most powerful form of marketing there is. (It's also true that corny, amateurish ads seize people's attention, but make sure that won't boomerang on your image.)

Join the trade. List your business with trade associations and in directories related to your industry. Purchase an advertisement in your industry's trade magazine. Trade magazines are among the most focused print advertisements you can find; their audiences are also laser targeted.

Make transit ads work. Advertise inside mass transit stations near your business. Like mobile advertising, many of these options advertise to people who may be far away from your business or visitors to your area. If location matters, choose wisely. However, unlike mobile advertising, you can generally deliver a longer sales message because you have prospects' undivided attention for a longer period of time.

Go after tourists. Advertise in tourist guides and/or on tourist maps. Depending on the kind of industry that you're in, this could be highly effective.

Use vehicles. Stick a few magnetic business cards to your vehicle that say "Take One." Include your logo, what you do, and your contact information. Or have your personal vehicle wrapped with your logo and slogan. Make it bright and hard to miss. You never know, when you're driving around, who might phone for your services.

As an entrepreneur, you probably never will give up trying to avoid bad break; to grow your business. We all know that getting new and potential customers to notice you is a never-ending battle. As you can see above, not all marketing techniques are complex or expensive. So call a company (or colleague) meeting, order lunch, and brainstorm, brainstorm, brainstorm. Offer rewards for ideas people contribute that are worth testing and that actually work. Try a new idea every week or two. Soon enough, you'll identify some winning marketing ploys and programs that will pay off in new sales and customers. The trick is to keep on keeping on. Good luck!

Afterword:
Where to Go from Here

IT MAY BE SAFE TO ASSUME that if you've just finished reading this book, you are one of two types of individuals. The *curious* reader may have been interested in learning how a potentially successful business could be envisioned, created and then finally launched to compete in the marketplace. For curious readers, these pages may have even sparked your imagination about becoming an entrepreneur one day. Curious readers have always shown interest in educating and informing themselves on a new topic and enhancing their knowledge base while doing so.

The *serious* reader may have chosen to read this book because he or she may have already decided to toss a hat in the ring and become an entrepreneur. Or perhaps, the business is launched and now additional tools, expert guidance, and real-world examples are vital for success. A serious reader never stops perusing every possible source for innovative ideas, the next greatest trend, or even a leg up on the competition.

Curious or serious, we hope that everyone who has read this second volume of our series found the material worthy of your time. Regardless of how or why you found us, we are glad you did.

For the guys who wrote this volume, and also founded the Expert Business Advice website, the philosophy was simple:

- Create material of substance and value that can continue to be expanded indefinitely for the benefit of the reader, the customer, and the business professional

- Deliver the best possible ideas, resources and guidance to those who seek it

- Take ownership of our work, stand by it, and be proud of it

Developing this material from several points of view and delivering it to people from diverse backgrounds and with multiple levels of experience was crucial for us. In fact, it was the only way we could imagine doing it.

Simply put, our goal with this series shares the same vision as our own company's slogan: "Experts Create | We Deliver | You Apply."

You may find you'd like to take our approach to explore other important aspects of starting and running a successful business. We especially would recommend these titles:

- A Crash Course in Starting a Business

- A Crash Course in Managing Your Business

- A Crash Course in Business Law Basics

The way forward begins here...

Acknowledgements

WE HAVE A LOT OF THANKS TO GIVE.

Scott wishes to thank his wife Kellin, his co-authors, his parents, the Girard Family, the Conway Family, the Edwards Family, the Seaman Family, the Warren Family (keep up the writing, Lea), the O'Keefe Family, everyone at Pinpoint Holdings Group, Barbara Stephens, Jack Chambless, Mary-Jo Tracy, Sandra McMonagle, Diane Orsini, Nathan Holic, Peter Telep, Pat Rushin, the Seminole Battalion, Dawn Price, and the Republic of Colombia (for the sweet, sweet brown nectar which fueled this project).

Mike wishes to thank his parents Tim and Gaye O'Keefe, his co-authors, Jamie, Kimberly Rupert, the O'Keefe Family, the Goldsberry Family, the Roy Family, the Hubert Family, the Murat Family, the Grant Family, the Girard Family, the Price Family, the Holycross Family, the most inspiring professor Jack Chambless, his two favorite authors Clive Cussler and Timothy Ferriss, and those individuals in Argentina (for making sure there is always Malbec on the table).

Marc wishes to thank his wife Dawn, his co-authors, his mom Lynda, the Price Family, the O'Bryan Family, the Smith Family, Jean Hughes, Kellin Girard, Mike Schiano, and his life-long mentor Howard Satin.

The authors would collectively like to thank Kathe Grooms and everyone at Nova Vista Publishing, everyone at Expert Business Advice, Jon Collier, and the Van Beekum Family: Dave, Melissa and the Sugar Gliders.

Glossary

Ad Swapping The exchange of advertising, most commonly between two businesses, for mutual benefit.

Advertising A form of communication used to encourage or incite an audience to continue or take some new action. Most commonly, the desired result is to guide consumer behavior with respect to a commercial offering.

Advertising Copy The text of an ad.

Agreement An arrangement reached between two or more parties in which the terms of a transaction or a course of action have been negotiated and documented. An agreement is typically legally enforceable as long as it is negotiated freely between legally competent parties.

Aerial Advertising A type of advertising that incorporates the use of aircraft, balloons or airships to create, transport, or display, advertising media. The media can be *static*, such as a banner, logo, lighted sign or sponsorship branding, or *dynamic*, such as animated lighted signage, skywriting or audio.

Attraction Marketing The use of marketing techniques specifically geared toward teaching the customer what you are doing and how your service or product will benefit them before they purchase it.

Audit An examination and verification of a business's financial and accounting records and supporting documents by a tax professional or governmental tax regulatory authority.

Bandit Signs	A guerrilla marketing tactic which places advertising posters or flyers in legal or illegal places. They get their name because they are so often mounted illegally. They are often removed not long after they are displayed.
Beta Testing	In product development, following internal alpha (first round) testing, external beta testing rates external users' acceptance and reveals flaws not previously caught. Versions of a new product, known as *beta versions*, are released to a limited audience outside of the company and feedback is captured. The process can be repeated after further refinements are made to ensure the product has few faults.
Blog	A personal journal published on the Internet consisting of discrete entries, called *posts*, typically displayed in reverse chronological order so the most recent post appears first.
Blue-Collar	A blue-collar employee is a member of the working class who usually performs manual labor. *Blue-collar work* may involve skilled or unskilled, manufacturing, construction, mechanical, maintenance, technical installation, and many other types of physical labor.
Brand	An identifying symbol, words, or mark that distinguishes a product or business from its competitors.
Brand Awareness	A marketing concept that enables marketers to quantify levels and track trends in consumer knowledge and awareness of a brand's existence.
Brand Development	The application of marketing techniques to the branding of a specific product, product line, or brand.
Brand Marketing	The act of marketing one's brand.
Brand Name	Often used interchangeably with *brand*, the phrase is more correctly used to specifically denote written or spoken linguistic elements of any product. In this context, however, a *brand name* is a type of trademark, as the brand name legally identifies the brand owner as the commercial source of products or services.

Branding	The act of distinguishing a product or business from its competitors by utilizing unique symbols, words, or marks.
Brick-and-Mortar Business	A company or portion of a company with a physical presence, as opposed to one that exists only virtually, on the Internet.
Brochures	Printed advertising pieces primarily used to introduce a business or organization, and inform about products and/or services, sales, and events to the target audience. They are typically distributed by mail, handed out personally, or placed in brochure racks.
Broker	An individual or firm who acts as an intermediary between a buyer and seller, typically charging a commission.
Business	A commercial activity aimed at making profits, engaged in as a means of occupation or income, or an entity which engages in such activities. Unlike non-profit organizations.
Business Directory	A website or printed listing of information which lists all businesses within given categories such as type of business, business sector, location, output, size, etc.
Buyer	In general terms, a person or entity who purchases some good or service from another.
Career Path	Often used interchangeably with *career*, a person's course or progress through a working life.
Certification	The process through which an official designation of some degree of reliability, knowledge, conformation to standards, etc. is obtained.
Charitable Activities	Acts of charity, generosity or philanthropy.
Closing a Sale	The resolute conclusion and completion of a sale. When one party agrees to pay, or pays, another for goods and/or services.
Cold-Calling	The practice of making unsolicited phone calls or visits to people you don't know in order to attract new business.

Colleague	Associate; typically a peer in a given workplace, rather than a social contact. Often used to blur hierarchical lines or when you don't know the working relationship of two people.
Competitor	A business or person that provides similar products or services.
Consultant	An external individual or company that provides information and guidance services to customers based on the consultant's field of expertise, usually for a fee.
Consumer	A person who buys products or services for personal use and not for manufacture or resale.
Consumer Behavior	The collective actions taken by consumers in deciding which goods and services hold the most value for meeting their wants and needs. It can include their searching, evaluation, selection, purchasing, consuming, and disposing of products.
Contract	A binding agreement between two or more parties for taking or refraining from taking some specified action(s) in exchange for lawful consideration.
Copyright	The exclusive right to produce and dispose of copies of a literary, musical, or artistic work.
Corporation	The most common form of business organization, and one which is given many legal rights as an entity separate from its owners. This form of business is characterized by the limited liability of its owners, the issuance of shares of easily transferable stock, and existence as a going concern.
Cost-Effective	Giving adequate and favorable value when compared with the original cost.
Culture	The breeding, education and sophistication of an individual or group of individuals. When applied to a business, its *corporate culture* describes the atmosphere, expectations and values that operate within a given company.
Customer Base	The group of customers that a business serves.

Customer Loyalty Program	A strategic marketing tactic aimed at increasing repeat purchases of customers and keeping them from crossing over to competitors, so that revenue goals are met or surpassed. Frequent flyer and buy-five-get-one-free-haircut programs are examples.
Customer Rapport	When a customer feels an affinity or bond with a business because she relates well with its operation and/or mission.
Customer Service	The delivery of service to customers before, during and after a purchase.
Database	An organized accumulation of data, today typically in digital form. The data are usually organized to depict relevant aspects of reality, in a way that supports processes requiring this information.
Demographics	Socioeconomic groups, characterized by age, income, sex, education, occupation, etc., that comprise a target market.
Direct Mail	The delivery of advertising material through postal mail to recipients.
Direct Selling	The marketing and selling of products directly to consumers.
Discount	To sell anything below its normal price.
Distributor	An entity which buys from a producer and then sells and delivers merchandise to retail stores, or acts as an intermediary in business. Sometimes called a *wholesaler* or *middleman*.
Downsizing	Diminishing the total number of employees at a company through terminations, retirements, or spinoffs.
Electronic Store	A retailer that exclusively sells electronic items and related components.
Email / Text Marketing	Marketing whereby advertisers deliver their messages and ads via text messages (SMSs) and emails.
Employee	A person hired to provide services to a company on a regular basis in exchange for compensation and who does not provide these services as part of an independently owned business.

Entrepreneur	An individual who starts his or her own business.
Expense	Any cost of conducting business resulting from revenue-generating activities.
Fair Price	A price for a product or service that is comparable to fair market value.
Fee	A charge for products delivered or services rendered.
Feedback	Usually evaluative information gathered from users or reviewers as part of a process in which information about past or current activities or products is used to improve in the future.
Geo-Targeting	A form of target marketing. If the location of a website visitor is known, it allows the delivery of different content to that visitor based on his or her location, such as country, region/state, city, metro code/zip code, organization, IP address, ISP, or other criteria.
Global Marketplace	Markets that develop between two or more regions, countries or nations.
Globalization	Processes of international integration, arising from increasing human connectivity and the interchange of worldviews, products, ideas, and other aspects of business culture.
Graphic Design	Commercial art, in which a creative process, usually involving a client and a designer, produces materials for a marketing plan, product or package design, advertisement, etc. It is aimed at conveying a specific message to a targeted audience.
Guarantee	To accept responsibility for an obligation if the entity with primary responsibility for the obligation fails to meet it.
Handouts	Something given or distributed free.
Human Resources	The division of a company which deals with "people" issues.
Impulse Buying	The act of purchasing without prior planning.
Industry	A basic category of corporate activity, frequently but not always associated with manufacturing. Thus, the auto industry, but also the film industry.

Intermediary	A third party who facilitates an arrangement or action between two other parties.
Internet	Commonly called a network of networks, the Internet is a global system of interconnected computer networks that use the standard Internet protocol suite to serve billions of users worldwide.
Internet Browser	A software application for retrieving, presenting and transferring information resources on the Internet.
Internet Forum	An online discussion site where people can hold conversations in the form of posted messages.
Internet Marketing	The marketing of products or services over the Internet. Also called web marketing, online marketing, webvertising, and e-marketing.
Interpersonal Communication	Communication among individuals.
Investor	An individual who commits monetary capital to investment products with the expectation of financial return.
Joint Promotions	Marketing that promotes two or more corporate entities or their output at the same time.
Joint Venture	A contractual agreement joining together two or more entities for the purpose of executing a particular business undertaking.
Key Players	Individuals who have a dramatic impact on the business, decision, or operations at hand.
Keyword	A word or identifier that has a specific meaning to the programming language.
Keyword Optimization	The process of using specifically selected keywords to improve the visibility of a website or a web page in a search engine's natural search results.
Law of Large Numbers	A law of economics that states that the more people you contact through marketing, the more people will purchase your products. However, common sense tells us that contacting the right people yields higher results.
Lead List	A pre-qualified list of prospects.

Lead	A suggestion that helps to direct or guide. In sales, a lead is a bit of information about a prospect who could become a customer.
Leads Group	A networking group formed to generate and share pre-qualified leads.
Licensing	Under defined conditions, the granting of permission to use intellectual property rights, such as trademarks, patents, or technology.
Life Coach	An individual who helps people identify and achieve personal goals.
Links	See *Hyperlinks*.
Logo	A graphic mark or emblem used by businesses, organizations and even individuals to aid and promote instant public recognition.
Manager	An individual responsible for one or more areas of a business, usually including supervision of others.
Manufactured Cost	The total cost of producing a product, including the direct labor costs, direct material costs, overhead costs, and any other expenses associated with production.
Manufacturing	The use of machines, tools and labor to produce goods for use or sale.
Market Penetration	Occurs when a business penetrates a market in which current products already exist.
Market Test	The limited sale of a product or service within a geographic region or to a demographic group to gauge its viability in a larger marketplace, prior to a wide-scale launch.
Marketing	The process by which products and services are announced and launched into the marketplace.
Marketing Budget	The amount of capital a business allocates for marketing expenses.
Marketing Collateral	The collection of media materials used to support and enhance the sales of a product or service.
Marketing Materials	Items used for the promotion of businesses, products or services.

Marketing Plan	A written document that defines the necessary actions to achieve one or more marketing objectives. It can be for a product or service, a brand, or a product line.
Marketing Tactic	Planned techniques and procedures for effectively approaching customers in pursuit of sales.
Marketplace	The area—actual, virtual or metaphorical—in which buying and selling take place.
Mass Media	Media technologies that are intended to reach a large audience via mass communication, e.g., national television networks, internationally published press, etc.
Media Platform	A software framework that manages media on a computer and through a network.
Mentor	A more experienced or more knowledgeable person who helps to guide a less experienced or less knowledgeable person.
Micro Blogging	A broadcast medium that differs from a traditional blog in that its content is typically smaller in both actual and aggregate file size.
Middleman	Intermediary between two commercial entities, commonly a manufacturer and a consumer.
Mobile Marketing	Marketing on or with a mobile device.
Network	An arrangement of connections.
Networking Groups	Groups designed to arrange connections among and through their members.
Newsletter	A distributed publication typically about one main topic that is of interest to its subscribers.
Non-Profit Company	An organization created to accomplish specified goals but without the intention of making profits, unlike a commercial organization. Its shareholders or trustees do not benefit financially. Some non-profits plow any potential profits back into their future budgets to avoid becoming profitable.
Occupation	Job or profession.
Offer	To express a desire to enter into an arrangement or contract with another person or entity.

Offering	A general term for the output of a business; the goods or services it sells.
Organization	A company, business, firm, or association.
Outsourcing	Arranging for work to be executed by people who are not the business's employees.
Placement	The selling of new securities. Can also refer to temporary employment with a company.
Premium Package	An upgraded amalgamation of products or services.
Premium Product	Generally, the top-of-the-line product that a business offers.
Press Release	A written or recorded message directed at members of the news media for the purpose of announcing something newsworthy. Also called a news release, media release, or press statement.
Price	The amount of money a seller expects to receive for a given product or service.
Print Media	Marketing material distributed in the form of text and images on paper, as distinct from other media (television, radio, Internet, etc.)
Private Labeling	A retailer's name, as used on a product sold by the retailer but manufactured by another company.
Product	The end result of the manufacturing process.
Productivity	The calculated amount of output per unit of input.
Projections	Quantitative estimates of prospective economic or financial performance.
Promotion	An activity, such as a sale or advertising campaign, designed to increase visibility or sales of a product.
Prospecting	The act of finding prospects.
Prospect, Prospective Customer	Potential buyers.
Psychological Factors	Factors driven by the emotional appeals of customers.
Public Relations	Efforts to establish, manage and maintain a business's image with the public.
Ratio	The result of one value divided by another.

Rebranding	Revamping and completing a total overhaul of a business's brand.
Referral	A person or business recommended to others.
Repeat Customer	A patron of a business who buys again and again.
Research	The process of gathering information.
Sales	Total amount collected for goods and services provided.
Sales Coach	An individual who helps salespeople identify and achieve professional sales goals.
Sales Objectives	Targeted goals of a salesperson or sales force.
Sales Team	A group of people who work at driving sales. Can be internal or external.
Search Engine Optimization (SEO)	The process of improving the popularity of a website or a web page in search engines' unpaid (*natural*) search results. In general, the earlier (or higher ranked on the search results page) and more frequently a site appears in the search results list, the more visitors it will receive from the search engine's users.
Selling Techniques	The body of specialized procedures and methods used by salespeople.
SEO Expert	An expert in Search Engine Optimization (SEO) techniques and procedures.
Service	A type of economic activity that is intangible, is not stored, and does not result in any kind of ownership. Examples are health care, training or entertainment.
Site	See *Website*.
Slogan	A memorable motto or phrase used repetitively as an expression of an idea or purpose, often connected with advertising.
Social Bookmarking	A method for Internet users to organize, store, manage and search for bookmarks (sometimes called *favorites*) of online resources.
Social Club	A group of people generally formed around a common interest, occupation or activity. Can also refer to the place where they meet.

Social Groups	Two or more people who interact with one another, share similar characteristics and collectively have a sense of unity.
Social Media	Web-based and mobile technologies used to turn communication into interactive dialogue among organizations, communities, and individuals. Social media are ubiquitously accessible, and enabled by scalable communication techniques.
Social Networking	See *Social Media*.
Social Tagging	A system of classification derived from the practice and method of collaboratively creating and managing tags to annotate and categorize online content.
Spam	Unsolicited advertising messages distributed indiscriminately in bulk. Most often it refers to Internet traffic, but it can be delivered by other media as well.
Sponsorship	Financial or other support, often for a specific event, program, or project, that may give the sponsor an opportunity to advertise.
Start-Up	1. The beginning of a new company or new product. 2. A new, usually small business that is just beginning its operations, especially a new business supported by venture capital and in a sector where new technologies are used.
Supply Chain	All the elements that combine to transform raw input into something an end-consumer can buy, including materials, knowledge, people, technology, transporters, distributors, retailers, etc. Can apply to intangible as well as tangible items.
Target Market	The most advantageous segment in which to offer a product or service to achieve a sales goal. Also called a market target.
Trade Journal	A publication whose focus is a given industry, sector, profession or type of trade.
Trademark	A distinctive name, symbol, motto, or design that legally identifies a business or its products and services, and sometimes prevents others from using identical or similar marks.

Trade Show	A marketing, fair-like event at which goods and services in a specific industry are exhibited, demonstrated and sold.
Trainer	An individual who trains or coaches others.
Trends	Increasingly frequent or widespread behavior. A financial trend is the current general direction of movement for prices or rates.
United States Patent and Trademark Office	An agency in the United States Department of Commerce that issues patents to inventors and businesses for their inventions, and trademark registration for product and intellectual property identification.
Under-Capitalized	An entity that lacks sufficient operating capital to perform well.
Union	An organization of workers joined to protect their common interests and improve their working conditions.
Website	A set of related web pages containing content such as text, images, video, audio, etc.
Wholesaler	A distributor or middleman who buys from producers and sells mainly to retailers and institutions, rather than directly to consumers.
Word-of-Mouth Advertising	Advertising distributed primarily informally, through the verbal communication of people.
Yield	The annual rate of return on an investment, expressed as a percentage.

Resources

ExpertBusinessAdvice.com

At **ExpertBusinessAdvice.com**, our goal is to become your complete resource for simple, easy-to-use business information and resources. Enjoy reading about techniques and processes necessary to develop and grow your business. **ExpertBusinessAdvice.com** offers an array of tools and resources to help you along the way by offering tutorials, downloadable templates, real-life examples, and customer support. You can even email us and a qualified member of our staff (yes, a real person!) will review your inquiry and get back to you within 24 hours. Now you can take charge of your professional growth and development, learn from others' success, and make a dramatic positive impact on your business. Learn the principles and practices that seasoned professionals use, at **ExpertBusinessAdvice.com,** for free!

THE WAY FORWARD BEGINS HERE…

Want to learn how to start a business? Are you looking for an additional income stream? No problem—we can get you started down the right path. Do you want to know how to plan, creating the necessary documents to obtain financing for your business? Maybe you just want to learn how experienced business leaders streamline financial models, maximize output, inspire managers, and incentivize employees, tapping the full range of resources available. Regardless of your needs, **ExpertBusinessAdvice.com** is here for you!

www.expertbusinessadvice.com

CRASH COURSE for ENTREPRENEURS

Many novice entrepreneurs have little more than a brilliant idea and a pocketful of ambition. They want to know *Now what?* This 12-title series tells *exactly what you must know*, in simple terms, using real-world examples. Each two-hour read walks you through a key aspect of being an entrepreneur and gives practical, seasoned, reader-friendly advice.

Whether your dream business is dog walking or high-tech invention, home-based or web-based, these books will save you time and trouble as you set up and run your new company. Collectively, these three young Florida-based serial entrepreneurs have successfully started seventeen new companies across a broad range of sectors and frameworks, including finance, international sourcing, medical products, innovative dot-com initiatives, and traditional brick-and-mortar companies.

A Crash Course for Entrepreneurs—From Expert Business Advice

Starting a Business – Everything you need to build a new business, starting from scratch.
Sales and Marketing – Solid guidance on successfully developing and promoting your business and its brand.
Managing Your Business – Proven techniques in managing employees and guiding your business in the right direction.
Business Finance Basics – Tax tips, funding, money management, basic accounting, and more!
Business Law Basics – A must-know overview on types of businesses, risks and liabilities, required documents, regulatory requirements, and the role of a business attorney. *Co-Author: Mark R. Moon, Esq.*
Franchising – A how-to guide for buying and running a franchise business.
Business Plans - Perhaps the most important thing you can do to get your start-up off to a great start is to create a strong business plan. Here's how!
Time and Efficiency – Wheel-spinning is the most destructive force in business. Make the most of your time to maximize income and motivate employees.
International Business – The world is a big place filled with billions of potential partners and customers. This guide offers tips to reach them all.
Supplemental Income – Can't commit full time? No problem! Here's how to make extra money in your spare time.
Social Media – This rapidly-growing networking and advertising medium is changing the world. Here's how to use it to grow your business.
Web-Based Business – The biggest, most valuable companies out there today are Internet businesses. Here's why, and how you can build one yourself.
Paperback and eBook format available. 160 pages, 6 ½" × 9" (16.5 × 23 cm), US$16.99, with extensive glossary and index.

www.expertbusinessadvice.com   www.novavistapub.com

Index

Tip: We suggest that you check the Glossary (pages 133-145) for definitions related to terms you want to look up in this index.

About the Authors

Scott L. Girard, Jr.

Editor-in-Chief, Expert Business Advice, LLC
Email: scott@expertbusinessadvice.com

Before joining Expert Business Advice, Scott was Executive Vice President of Pinpoint Holdings Group, Inc., where he directed multiple marketing and advertising initiatives. Scott was a key player for the Group, negotiating and facilitating the sourcing logistics for the commercial lighting industry division, which supplied clients such as Gaylord Palms, Ritz Carlton, Marriott, Mohegan Sun, and Isle of Capri with large-scale lighting solutions. His vision and work were also pivotal in the growth and development of Bracemasters International, LLC.

Scott has degrees in Business Administration and English Writing and is a published contributor to various periodicals on the topics of economics and politics. He is also a co-author and series editor of *A Crash Course for Entrepreneurs* book series. A graduate of the United States Army Officer Candidate School, Scott is a combat veteran, having served a tour in Kuwait and Iraq as an infantry platoon leader in support of Operation Iraqi Freedom and Operation New Dawn.

Originally from Glendale, California, Scott now lives in St. Petersburg, Florida with his wife. Scott is a regular contributor to www.expertbusinessadvice.com. His side projects include a collection of fiction short stories and scripts for two feature films. His motto: "Words have meaning."

Michael F. O'Keefe

Chief Executive Officer, Expert Business Advice, LLC
Email: mike@expertbusinessadvice.com

In 2004, Mike founded O'Keefe Motor Sports, Inc. (OMS Superstore), eventually growing it into the largest database of aftermarket automotive components available for online purchase in the world. Currently, aside from his position at Expert

Business Advice, LLC, Mike is President of Pinpoint Holdings Group, Inc. and Vice President of Marketing for Bracemasters International, LLC.

At Pinpoint, Mike's focus is building a strong base for understanding the global marketplace. He also plays a key role in facilitating the logistics of the commercial lighting branch of the company, bridging between Pinpoint's office in Wuxi, China, and their commercial clients—hotel chains such as Gaylord Palms, Ritz Carlton, Marriott, Mohegan Sun and Isle of Capri.

Recently, Mike's passion and talents for cutting-edge business techniques and practices have led to the exponential growth of Bracemasters. By developing web-based marketing strategies and E-commerce initiatives, as well as formatting on-line documents that enabled the company to reach a vast number of current and potential patient-customers, Mike increased Bracemasters' website viewership by 17,000% in two years.

Originally from Delavan, Wisconsin, Mike now lives in Orlando, Florida. He is a regular contributor to www.expertbusinessadvice.com. His motto: "Rome did not create a great empire by having meetings; they did it by killing all those who opposed them."

Marc A. Price

Director of Operations, Expert Business Advice, LLC
Email: marc@expertbusinessadvice.com

Marc has collaborated with the United States Federal Government, United States Military, major non-profit organizations, and some of the largest corporations in America, developing and implementing new products, services and educational programs. Equally skilled in Business-to-Business and Business-to-Consumer functions, Marc has facilitated product positioning, branding and outreach efforts on many different platforms for the organizations he has worked with.

As an entrepreneur, Marc has successfully directed the launch of seven different companies, ranging from traditional brick-and-mortar establishments to innovative dot-com initiatives. Four were entertainment production companies (sound, lighting, staging, logistics, talent, entertainment), one was a business services company serving small companies, one was concerned with business and land acquisition, and two were website and business consulting services. Using his expertise in organizational management and small business development, Marc's latest focus is on working with new entrepreneurs and small-to-medium-sized businesses in emerging industries.

As an accomplished public speaker and writer, Marc has appeared on nationally syndicated television and radio networks, in national print publications, and has been the subject of numerous interviews and special-interest stories. Marc is a regular contributor to www.expertbusinessadvice.com.

Marc received his Bachelor of Science in Organizational Management from Ashford University. He and his wife divide time between Orlando, Florida and elsewhere, including an active schedule of international travel. His motto: "You can't build a reputation on what you are going to do."—Henry Ford

Business Efficiency Resources

Get More Done Seminars

Grooms Consulting Group, a sister company to Nova Vista Publishing, offers proven training that saves professionals one month or more of time wasted on email, information and meeting inefficiency.

• 83% of all professionals are overloaded by email – we can save up to 3 weeks a year, per person
• 92% want to improve their information storage system – we can make searches 25% faster and more successful
• 43% of all meeting time is wasted – we can save up to another 3 weeks per year, per person

"We saved 15 days a year!"
Matt Koch, Director of Productivity
Capital One Financial Services

Three Two-Hour Modules: We offer three powerful seminars: **Get Control of Email, Get Control of Info**, and **Get Control of Meetings**.
They can be delivered in any combination you wish and can be customized.
Who Should Attend? Anyone who handles email, stores information, and attends meetings. Leaders leverage their position for added impact.
Delivery Options: Seminar, keynote speech, webinar, e-learning, and executive coaching.
Return on Investment (ROI): We can measure the impact of every session on participants with five-minute online pre- and post-surveys. We deliver a report that shows time saved, productivity gained, participant satisfaction, and other significant impacts.

Special pricing is available for groups.

Three *Get More Done* Modules: Combine and Customize as You Wish

1. GET CONTROL OF EMAIL
• Pump up your productivity by eliminating unnecessary email
• De-clutter your jammed inbox
• Write more effective messages
• Discover time-saving Outlook® / Lotus® tech tips
• Improve email etiquette and reduce legal liability
• Choose the best communication tool

2. GET CONTROL OF INFORMATION
• Get organized, once and for all
• Never lose a document again
• File and find your information in a flash; make shared drives productive
• Make better decisions with the right information
• Create an ordered, stress-free folder structure throughout your system

3. GET CONTROL OF MEETINGS
• Meet less and do more through virtual and other advanced options
• Reduce costs, boost productivity and go green with improved, efficient virtual meetings
• Run engaging, productive live meetings
• Discover time-saving e-calendar tips
• Keep every meeting productive and on track, make follow-ups easy

Satisfaction Guaranteed
We guarantee that the vast majority of your people will rate our seminars "excellent" or "good," or your money back.

"A huge hit with our people!"
Joel Burkholder
Regional Program Coordinator – ACLCP

Contact: Kathe Grooms
kgrooms@groomsgroup.com

Two Must-Read Books For Entrepreneurs

Win-Win Selling: Turning Customer NEEDS into SALES

Differentiating your company's products and services is a big challenge today. But a company's sales force can become a significant differentiator, and gain sustainable advantages, if it adopts the Counselor approach. A win-win mind and skill set, based on trust, problem-solving and side-by-side work between seller and customer, makes buying easy. And because the seller stays by the customer after the sale, the door opens for long-term, expanding business.

Fortune 500 global and other companies in 30 countries have used Wilson Learning's Counselor approach for years with astonishing success. The book gives the million-plus people who have taken Wilson Learning's The Counselor Salesperson workshop a refresher, and gives others a powerful sales process. The Foreword is by Larry Wilson, author of One Minute Salesperson and founder of Wilson Learning (1965). It's an indispensable book for salespeople and sales managers, who agree it's solid, practical and really works.

"The Counselor Approach enhanced our leadership position by helping our sales and marketing organization discover what is most important in our marketplace. As a result, we are adding value to our customers as a means of advocating for the patient."

Dan Schlewitz, Vice President Sales, Medtronic CRM

Win-Win Selling (ISBN Third Edition 978-90-77256-34-3)
160 pages, softcover, 160 × 230 cm (6" × 9")
Suggested retail price: € 18.95, US$18.95
Models, charts, anecdotes, an index and other resources.

Versatile Selling: Adapting Your Style So Your Customers Say "Yes!"

This book presents the concepts and tools of The Social Styles Handbook, specifically adapted for the needs of salespeople. The powerful yet simple skill of Versatility—the ability to read and adapt to the natural behavior of your customers—makes them feel comfortable and ready to buy, and has been proven to increase sales measurably.

Learn to assess your own Social Style (Driver, Analytical, Amiable, or Expressive) and the style of your customer. That way you know how your customer wants to be treated, and you can adapt your own behavior to the customer's specific needs and expectations. You will also know how to respond to and decrease unproductive tension and get back to productive collaboration, because you know how to handle Back-Up Behaviors of customers of different styles. No matter what sales process you use, this book will help you work better with every customer.

"The concepts in Versatile Selling changed my career and my life. I've been through a lot of training, and even after 33 years in sales I try to keep learning. Social Styles, Versatility and the Wilson Learning approach to sales have given me the solid foundation I needed to achieve the success I've had."

W. Jacques Gibbs, Investment Advisor

Versatile Selling (ISBN 90-77256-03-2)
160 pages, softcover, 160 × 230 cm (6" × 9"), € 18.95, US$18.95
Models, charts, anecdotes, an index and other resources.

Now available in eBook formats!
www.novavistapub.com

CAREERS
I Just Love My Job!
Roy Calvert, Brian Durkin, Eugenio Grandi and Kevin Martin, in the Quarto Consulting Library (ISBN 978-90-77256-02-2, softcover, 192 pages, $19.95)

Taking Charge of Your Career
Leigh Bailey (ISBN 978-90-77256-13-8, softcover, 96 pages, $14.95)

LEADERSHIP AND INNOVATION
Grown-Up Leadership
Leigh Bailey and Maureen Bailey (ISBN 978-90-77256-09-1, softcover, 144 pages, $18.95)

Grown-Up Leadership Workbook
Leigh Bailey (ISBN 978-90-77256-15-2, softcover, 96 pages, $14.95)

Leading Innovation
Brian McDermott and Gerry Sexton (ISBN 978-90-77256-05-3, softcover, 160 pages, $18.95)

Time Out for Leaders
Donald Luce and Brian McDermott (ISBN 978-90-77256-30-5 softcover, $14.95)

SALES
Time Out for Salespeople
Nova Vista Publishing's Best Practices Editors, (ISBN 978-90-77256-14-5 hardcover with marker ribbon, 272 pages, $19.95; ISBN 978-90-77256-31-2 softcover, 272 pages, $14.95)

Get-Real Selling, Revised Edition
Michael Boland and Keith Hawk (ISBN 978-90-77256-32-9, softcover, 144 pages, $18.95)

COMMUNICATION
Social Styles Handbook, Revised Edition
Wilson Learning Library (ISBN 978-90-77256-33-6, softcover, 192 pages, $18.95)

SCIENCE PARKS, ECONOMICS, ECOLOGY OF INNOVATION
What Makes Silicon Valley Tick?
Tapan Munroe, Ph.D., with Mark Westwind, MPA (ISBN 978-90-77256-28-2, softcover, 192 pages, $19.95)

Visit www.novavistapub.com for sample chapters, reviews, links and ordering. eBooks are now available too!